CRITICAL INCIDENT STRESS MANAGEMENT (CISM): Group Crisis Intervention

3rd Edition Revised

Jeffrey T. Mitchell, Ph.D., C.T.S.
University of Maryland Baltimore County

and

George S. Everly, Jr., Ph.D., F.A.P.M.
Loyola College in Maryland
and
The Johns Hopkins University

About the Authors

George S. Everly, Jr., Ph.D., is Chairman of the Board Emeritus and Representative to the United Nations for the International Critical Incident Stress Foundation, a non-profit organization that provides education, training, and consultation in the areas of crisis intervention, psychological trauma and disaster mental health throughout the world. The largest organization of its kind in the world, the Foundation coordinates an international network of more than 300 crisis response teams. Dr. Everly also serves on the adjunct faculties of Loyola College in Maryland, and The Johns Hopkins University. Dr. Everly is Distinguished Visiting Professor at the Universidad de Flores de Buenos Aires and is Senior Research Advisor, Social Development Office, Office of His Highness the Amir of Kuwait, State of Kuwait. Prior these appointments, Dr. Everly was a Harvard Scholar, Harvard University; a Visiting Lecturer in Medicine for, Harvard Medical School; and Chief Psychologist and Director of Behavioral Medicine for the Johns Hopkins' Homewood Hospital Center.

Considered a leading authority on crisis intervention, human stress, and psychological trauma,, Dr. Everly has been awarded the Fellow' Medal of the Academy of Psychosomatic Medicine, and the Professor's Medal of the Universidad de Weiner, Lima, Peru. Dr. Everly has been elected member of the Green Cross Foundation's Academy of Traumatology and elected a Master Traumatologist by the Traumatology Institute of the Florida State University. In addition, he has been elected a Fellow of the American Institute of Stress, and is a Diplomate and Advisory Board Member of the Academy of Experts in Traumatic Stress. He is the author, co-author, or editor of 12 textbooks and more than 125 professional papers. Among his texts are **Critical Incident Stress Management, 2nd Edition** (Chevron, 1999), **Psychotraumatology** (Plenum, 1995), **Critical Incident Stress Debriefing** (Chevron, 1995), **A Clinical Guide to the Treatment of the Human Stress Response** (Plenum, 1989), **Controlling Stress and Tension, 5th Edition** (Prentice-Hall, 1996), and **Personality and Its Disorders,** with Theodore Millon (Wiley, 1985).

Jeffrey T. Mitchell, Ph.D., CTS, ICISF's co-founder, is a Clinical Associate Professor of the Emergency Health Services Department at the University of Maryland. He developed the Critical Incident Stress management (CISM) program which includes the specific group crisis intervention process known as Critical Incident Stress Debriefing (CISD). CISM is utilized by more than 700 communities throughout the United States and in twenty-three other nations. Dr. Mitchell co-founded the International Critical Incident Stress Foundation and he is the senior author of the following books: **Human Elements Training; CISD: An Operations Manual, Second Edition (Revised); Emergency Response to Crisis** and **Emergency Services Stress.** He has more than 250 other publications on critical incident stress, crisis intervention and the treatment of stress in emergency personnel. He is a recipient of the Bronze Medal from the Australian Red Cross.

Authors' Note:

The contents of this workbook are provided as a set of general guidelines only, they are not intended to be used as a self-help manual, nor a substitute for psychotherapy or professional mental health guidance. Similarly, this manual may not be used as a substitute for formal training and supervision. When in doubt, always consult a licensed mental health professional.

TABLE OF CONTENTS

Course Schedule .... 5 - 12

Section One   Critical Incident Stress Management (CISM) and
Emergency Mental Health .... 13 - 32

Section Two   Stress .... 33 - 38

Section Three   Stress Management .... 39 - 46

Section Four   Traumatic Stress .... 47 - 54

Section Five   Demobilizations .... 55 - 60

Section Six   Crisis Management Briefings .... 61 - 70

Section Seven   Defusings .... 71 - 76

Section Eight   Critical Incident Stress Debriefing (CISD) .... 77 - 94

Section Nine   Common Mistakes .... 95 - 100

Section Ten   Narrative and Statistical Reviews .... 101 - 130

Section Eleven   CISM Team Formation .... 131 - 134

Section Twelve   CIS Information Sheets .... 135 - 138

Appendix   Phases of the Airline Mass Disaster .... 139 - 146

IMPORTANT CISM TRAINING RESOURCES

1. Everly, G. S. and Mitchell, J. T. (1999). *Critical Incident Stress Management: A New Era and Standard of Care in Crisis Intervention, 2nd Edition.* Ellicott City, MD: Chevron Publishing Corporation.

2. Mitchell, J.T. and Everly, G.S., Jr. (2001). *Critical Incident Stress Debriefing (CISD): An Operations Manual 3rd Edition.* Ellicott City, MD: Chevron Publishing Corporation.

3. Mitchell, J.T. and Everly, G.S., Jr. (1994). *Human Elements Training.* Ellicott City, MD: Chevron Publishing Corporation.

4. *CISD: Critical Incident Stress Debriefing: Techniques of Debriefing* (1991). Video Tape by J.T. Mitchell. St. Louis, MO: Mosby Publishing.

5. *International Journal of Emergency Mental Health.* Ellicott City, MD. Chevron Publishing Corporation.

Recommended Course Schedule
Critical Incident Stress Management:
Group Crisis Intervention

Note: Instructor style, the use of audio visuals to enhance the presentation of material, group needs and questions from the participants may impact the exact timing of the presentation of this course. There may also be alterations in the order of the material presented. Timing alterations as well as alterations in the order of presentation are certainly acceptable in a course of this nature. The material presented in the course, however, should comply with the topics outlined in the course schedule printed below. We hope the course is helpful to you and those you serve. Thank you for your interest in CISM.
- Jeffrey T. Mitchell Ph.D., CTS and George S. Everly, Jr., Ph.D.

Day 1

Registration and course materials distribution

Welcome and introductory remarks
- Instructor introduction
- Course overview
- Ground rules for the course
- Special conditions and cautions
- Identification of professions present
- ICISF and its roles and services

The nature of stress
- General stress
- Cumulative stress
- Critical Incident Stress (CIS)
- Post Traumatic Stress Disorder (PTSD)
- Signs and symptoms of stress reactions
- Benefits of stress management programs

Crisis
- Definition of crisis
- Three characteristics of crisis
    a) Disrupted homeostasis
    b) Coping mechanisms fail
    c) Evidence of impairment

- Crisis intervention definition and description
- Five main goals of crisis intervention
    a) Stabilization
    b) Mitigation
    c) Mobilization of resources
    d) Normalization
    e) Restoration to function
- Crisis intervention is support, not psychotherapy
- Crisis intervention is prevention oriented, not cure oriented
- Fundamental principles of crisis intervention
    a) Simplicity
    b) Brevity
    c) Pragmatism
    d) Innovative
    e) Proximity
    f) Immediacy
    g) Expectancy
- Critical Incident Stress Management (CISM) - overview

Traumatic events likely to cause Critical Incident Stress
- "The Terrible Ten"
    a) Suicide of a colleague, friend, family member
    b) Line of duty death; death at the workplace
    c) Serious line of duty/workplace injury
    d) Disaster / multi-casualty incident
    e) Police shootings / accidental killing or wounding of an innocent person / events with extreme threat to the participants
    f) Significant events involving children
    g) Prolonged incidents especially with a loss
    h) Events in which the victims are relatives of or are known to the operations personnel
    i) Events with excessive media interest
    j) Any significant event capable of causing considerable emotional distress in those who are exposed to it.

CISM
- Overview of the core interventions of CISM:
    a) Pre-incident education and preparation
    b) One-on-one crisis intervention
    c) Demobilization (public safety, disaster response personnel)
    d) Crisis management briefings (large groups of primary victims)
    e) Defusing
    f) Critical Incident Stress Debriefing (CISD)
    g) Significant other/ Family support
    h) Organizational/Community consultations
    i) Pastoral crisis intervention
    j) Follow-up services and or referrals

Brief overview of the supportive research behind:
    a) Critical Incident Stress Debriefing (CISD)
    b) Critical Incident Stress Management (CISM)

Overview and description of the group processes of:
    a) Demobilization
    b) Crisis Management Briefing (CMB)
    c) Defusing
    d) Critical Incident Stress Debriefing (CISD)
- Similarities between the four group interventions
- Differences between the four group interventions

Demobilization
- Definition
- Description
- Used for large scale incidents
- Used in prolonged incidents
- Provided only one time after the first exposure to the event
- Passive process. Presenter provides information
- Questions or comments from the participants are invited, but it is rare that participants would ask questions or make

comments. They are usually too tired from the situation to engage in a discussion.

- Immediately after release from first exposure to the event
- The demobilization is only 10 minutes of information then 20 minutes of food and rest
- Instructor should provide a brief demonstration of how a demobilization is conducted

The Crisis Management Briefing (CMB)

- Definition
- Description (45-75 minutes)
- Used with large groups of civilians, schools, businesses, industrial groups, community groups, military
- Very much like the demobilization for operations personnel, but may involve more questions and comments from the non-operations participants
- Primary purpose is to present information and reassurance, and instructions to the participants

Defusing

- Definition
- Description
- When is a defusing utilized?
- Immediacy
- Mission is complete
- Uses a team approach
- Peers may do without mental health professional
- Small group
- Active group discussion
- Short in duration (20-45 minutes is typical)
- Components
  a) Introduction
  b) Exploration
  c) Information

Demonstration of defusing
- Introduction
- Instructions on what to look for
- Discussion after the demonstration

"Introductory remarks" exercise in groups of four
- Instructions to the groups
- Discussion of experiences of group participants

Defusing exercise in groups of eight
- Presentation of a standard scenario by the instructor
- Two team members chosen to play the roles of a defusing team
- One person is chosen to be a silent observer for the purposes of the role-play. The observer monitors the role-play and takes notes so he or she can provide feedback at the end of the exercise. Note: observer / note takers are only used in a role-play; *never* in a real defusing or a debriefing.
- Five people play out various roles in the role play
- The observer / note taker provides feedback to the group especially to the people who played out the helper roles in the defusing role-play.
- General discussion after the exercise with question and answer period conducted by the course instructor

End of day one

Day 2

CISD video with brief discussion following the video

Detailed point-by-point coverage of the CISD process
- Definition
- Overview
- Structure
- When to use a CISD
- Signs that a CISD is indicated
- Automatic CISD vs. discretionary CISD
- Team selection
- Timing
- Phase by phase description of the CISD
- Likely problems
- Preparing the team
- Gathering intelligence
- Role of peer support personnel
- Door keeper role
- Role of mental health professional
- Role of clergy in a CISD
- Etc.

Option #1 Selection of role players for a demonstration CISD (10-12 people).

Break (Instructor will meet with the role players to assign roles and lay out the scenario. Each role player will be instructed on how to play out the role that was assigned to him or her. Some will be "team" members others will be those playing a role of someone who is participating the debriefing.)

Demonstration CISD
- Discussion of the demonstration
- Question and answer period
- Course conclusion
- Course evaluations

OR

Option #2 Divide the course participants into groups of 10-12 people in each group. Present each group with the same scenario. Two people play the role of the CISM team that is going to provide the CISD. The others play out roles of people who are in need of the debriefing.

Break (The groups prepare their roles and the role players who are going to be the "CISD team" prepare separately for how they are going to conduct the CISD. It is best not to use an observer in this role-play. In this option, everyone should have a role to play within the scenario.)

Role-play in groups.
- Instructor moves from group to group and listens, stops the role-play temporarily and points out things that would help the group members.
- Feedback from all of the group members to their own "helpers"
- Discussion of the group CISD experience
- Question and answer period
- Course conclusion
- Course evaluation

END of course

Notes

Section One

CRITICAL INCIDENT STRESS MANAGEMENT AND EMERGENCY MENTAL HEALTH

THE CORE CONCEPTS: CRISIS INTERVENTION AND CRITICAL INCIDENT STRESS MANAGEMENT

There can be little doubt that the inability to communicate in a common parlance inhibits progress. From the Biblical references to the Tower of Babel, the reputation of Humpty Dumpty by Alice in the literary classics "Through the Looking Glass," and even the observation by pioneering physician George Engel that a substantive issue in rationale discourse is the need to use terms consistently, we see that a key foundation of knowledge itself is the definition of terms. With this thought in mind we offer the following definitions that will serve to guide the reader.

CRISIS - a response to an event wherein 1) an individual's psychological homeostasis is disrupted, 2) one's usual coping mechanisms have failed, and 3) there is evidence of distress and significant functional impairment, (Everly and Mitchell, 1999).

CRITICAL INCIDENT - the event which has the potential to engender a crisis response. This term is often confused with the crisis response itself.

CRISIS INTERVENTION - Psychological "first-aid." As physical first-aid is to surgery, crisis intervention is to psychotherapy. The functional goals of crisis intervention are:

1) Symptom stabilization, i.e., prevent the symptoms of distress/impairment from worsening.
2) Symptom reduction
3) Re-establish functional capacity, or
4) Seek further assessment and/or a higher level of care (Everly, 1999).

CRITICAL INCIDENT STRESS MANAGEMENT (CISM) - a comprehensive, integrated multi-component crisis intervention system (Everly and Mitchell, 1999). CISM consists of a set of core interventions (see Figure 1) useful for public safety applications, schools, businesses, industry, and communities.

1) Pre-crisis planning/education
2) Individual crisis intervention (one-on-one)
3) Small group crisis intervention - Defusing
4) Small group crisis intervention - CISD
5) Large group crisis intervention - Demobilizations (for public safety, rescue, disaster personnel)
6) Large group crisis intervention - Crisis Management Briefing (CMB) for civilian populations, schools, businesses, communities, etc.
7) Organizational consultation
8) Family crisis intervention
9) Pastoral crisis intervention
10) Mechanisms for follow-up and referral

Figure 1
Critical Incident Stress Management
(CISM; Everly & Mitchell, 1999)

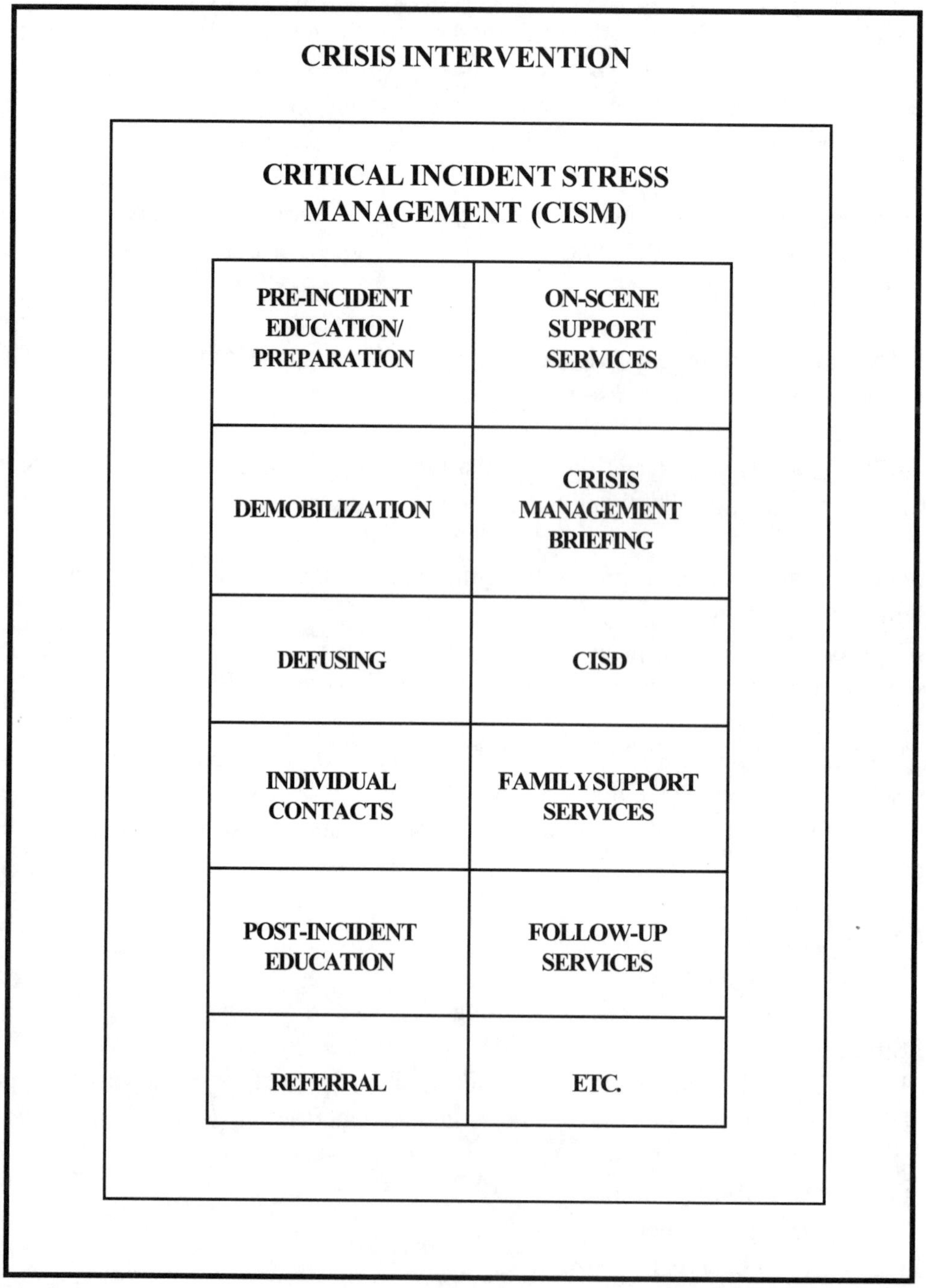

CRISIS INTERVENTION

CRITICAL INCIDENT STRESS MANAGEMENT (CISM)

PRE-INCIDENT EDUCATION/ PREPARATION	ON-SCENE SUPPORT SERVICES
DEMOBILIZATION	CRISIS MANAGEMENT BRIEFING
DEFUSING	CISD
INDIVIDUAL CONTACTS	FAMILY SUPPORT SERVICES
POST-INCIDENT EDUCATION	FOLLOW-UP SERVICES
REFERRAL	ETC.

A BRIEF HISTORICAL TIMELINE
FOR CRISIS INTERVENTION

As any field evolves, there are "milestones," which mark significant events in the evolution of that field. The field of crisis intervention represents an endeavor characterized by the provision of urgent and acute psychological "first aid." While clearly not the practice of psychotherapy, the goals of crisis intervention are the stabilization of symptoms of distress, reduction of symptoms of distress, and improvement in adaptive independent functioning, or facilitation of access to higher levels of support. Listed below are some of the most important milestones in the development of this important area of applied mental health.

1906 .... National Save-A-Life League for suicide prevention;

World War I .... The first empirical evidence that early intervention reduces chronic psychiatric morbidity;

World War II .... The processes of immediacy, proximity, and expectancy identified as important "active ingredients" in effective emergency psychological response;

1944 .... Lindemann's observations of grief reactions to the Coconut Grove fire begins "modern era" of crisis intervention;

late 1950s .... Community suicide prevention programs proliferated;

1963/64 .... Caplan's three tiers of preventive psychiatry implemented within the newly created community mental health system (i.e. primary prevention, secondary prevention, tertiary prevention)

late 1960s/ early 1970s .... Crisis intervention principles applied to reduce the need for hospitalization of potentially "chronic" populations

1974 .... early work on crisis and stress in emergency services personnel

1980 .... Formal nosological recognition of posttraumatic stress disorder (PTSD) in DSM-III "legitimizes" an examination of crisis and traumatic events as threats to long-term mental health;

1982 .... Air Florida 90 air disaster in Washington D.C. prompts re-examination of psychological support for emergency response personnel; first mass disaster use of the group crisis intervention Critical Incident Stress Debriefing (CISD) which was originally formulated in 1974;

1986 .... "Violence in the workplace" era begins with death of 13 postal workers on the job;

1989 .... International Critical Incident Stress Foundation (ICISF) formalizes an international network of over 350 crisis response teams trained in a standardized and comprehensive crisis intervention model (CISM);

1992 .... American Red Cross initiates formal training for the establishment of a nationwide disaster mental health capability; Hurricane Andrew tests the new mental health function;

1993 .... Social Development Office (Amiri Diwan), ICISF, Kuwait University, and others implement a nationwide crisis intervention system for post-war Kuwait;

1993 .... First World Trade Center bombing;

1994 .... DSM-IV recognizes Acute Stress Disorder;

1995 .... Bombing of the Federal Building in Oklahoma City underscores need for crisis services for rescue personnel, as well as civilians;

1996 .... TWA 800 mass air disaster emphasizes the need for emergency mental health services for families of the victims of traumas and disasters;

1996 .... OSHA 3148-1996 recommends comprehensive violence/crisis intervention programs in healthcare and social service agencies;

1996 .... Aviation Disaster Family Assistance Act;

1997 .... Gore Commission recommends crisis services for airline industry; ICISF gains United Nations affiliation in 1997;

1997 .... AFI 44-153 mandates establishment of crisis programs for US Air Force bases worldwide;

1998 .... OSHA 3153-1998 recommends crisis intervention programs for late-night retail stores;

1999 .... COMDINST 1754.3 requires the establishment of a CISM team for each US Coast Guard region;

1999 .... DoD DIRECTIVE 6490.5 establishes policy and responsibilities for developing Combat Stress Control (CSC) programs throughout the US military;

1999 .... Mass casualty shooting in Colorado high school leads to a re-examination of youth and school violence issues and an increase in the establishment of school crisis response programs;

2000 .... Increased international concern for nuclear, biological, and/or chemical terrorism includes planning for mental health consequences.

These aforementioned milestones in the historical development of the field of crisis intervention have served to shape its nature and provide useful insight into its current status.

Early Psychological Intervention: State-of-the Art

I. NIMH (2002) - The recent NIMH recommendations entitled the *Mental Health and Mass Violence Report* (NIMH, 2002) addressed two important issues relevant to the field of crisis intervention:

1. Should early psychological intervention (within 4 weeks of the event) be practiced?

2. If so, what should such an intervention consist of?

The consensus work group agreed:

1. While most survivors of mass disasters and violence should be expected to experience a normal recovery, there is a rationale for providing early psychological interventions to those in need.

2. The intervention itself should be a phasic, integrated multicomponent intervention system.

3. Follow-up services should be considered for:

        a. the bereaved.
        b. those with preexisting psychiatric disorders.
        c. those who required medical / surgical intervention.
        d. those with acute stress disorder.
        e. those for whom exposure was especially chronic or intense.
        f. those who request it.

4. Early intervention services may be implemented by mental health professionals, the clergy, medical and nursing professionals, para professionals and community volunteers.

II. Cochrane Review (2002) - Single session stand alone, one-on-one "debriefing" should be discontinued. No conclusions were made regarding "group debriefings" or mass disaster interventions.

III. Employee Assistance Professionals Association (EAPA) (2002) - Workplace based employee assistance programs should develop disaster plans. Plans should provide for a <u>continuum</u> of services to include pre-incident preparation, acute response services and follow-up services. Risk assessment, policy development, CISM training and supervisory CIS training were included as part of pre-incident preparation. Large group, small group (CISD) and individual crisis intervention services were included in the continuum of post incident response interventions.

IV. P. Ritchie (2002) - Management of Critical Incident Stress in a military environment. Small group crisis intervention (CISD) should be implemented within the context of a multi-component intervention system with 1 : 1 counseling provided in addition to, or instead of, the CISD as the needs of the situation demand.

CRITICAL INCIDENT STRESS MANAGEMENT (CISM)

INTRODUCTION

In the evolution of crisis intervention, Critical Incident Stress Management (CISM) represents a new generation of collective intervention technologies. More specifically, CISM represents an integrated, comprehensive multicomponent crisis intervention program spanning the complete crisis continuum (Everly and Mitchell, 1997). "Its comprehensive nature gives it the flexibility to be applied to a wide diversity of settings and constituent groups" (Everly and Mitchell, 1997, p. 9). CISM is a crisis intervention system useful for schools, businesses, industrial, as well as public safety and mass disaster applications.

As anyone who has attempted the game of golf knows, it requires the skillful utilization of numerous and diverse golf clubs to function effectively amidst the challenges of the golf course. Similarly, as anyone who has attempted the mitigation of acute human distress knows, it requires the skillful utilization of numerous and diverse crisis intervention technologies to function effectively amidst the challenges of human crisis. Thus, in crisis intervention as in the game of golf, a multidimensional multicomponent approach is required.

The notion that crisis intervention should be multidimensional is not new. Bordow and Porritt (1979) cogently demonstrated that multicomponent crisis intervention was more effective for traffic accident victims than "one shot" single session interventions. Single interventions were, however, more effective than no intervention at all. Raphael (1986) suggested the use of a broader spectrum approach to crisis intervention, especially for utilization with emergency response personnel. But it was Mitchell (1983, 1988) who first suggested that a multicomponent crisis intervention program should be utilized with the potential secondary victims of crisis and trauma, e.g., emergency services personnel. Initially, this multicomponent approach to crisis intervention was generically referred to as Critical Incident Stress Debriefing and collectively included interventions such as individual crisis support techniques, pre-crisis education, a 3-step immediate small group discussion called defusing, a 7-step more structured group discussion called formal Critical Incident Stress Debriefing (CISD), and follow-up psychological services. Mitchell (1988) later expanded this multicomponent crisis intervention approach to include mental preparation and a psychological decompression technique called demobilization for very large groups, which is used after mass disasters.

As might be imagined, considerable operational confusion resulted from the semantic overlap in the use of the term Critical Incident Stress Debriefing where in one context it was used to describe a collective genre of crisis intervention techniques, yet in another context it was used to describe a specific formalized 7-step group discussion. In 1993, Mitchell and Everly authored a seminal text on multicomponent crisis intervention entitled *Critical Incident Stress Debriefing: An Operations Manual*. Although entitled Critical Incident Stress Debriefing, the text clearly delineated a broad-based multicomponent crisis intervention system that consisted of over 10 crisis intervention technologies. Finally, in 1997, Everly (Everly and Mitchell, 1997) consolidated and functionally integrated the multicomponent system initially described by Mitchell (1983, 1988) into a core component crisis intervention program using the term Critical Incident Stress Management (CISM), as previously proposed by Mitchell, to designate the new dynamic multicomponent crisis intervention system. The core components of CISM are listed in Table 1.

CISM is designed to be "comprehensive." By using the term comprehensive, we mean that the CISM program spans the entire 3 phases of the crisis spectrum: 1) the pre-crisis phase, 2) the acute crisis phase, and 3) the post-crisis phase (Everly and Mitchell, 1997). We agree with the recommendation of the British Psychological Society (1990) that crisis intervention techniques should be multi-componential and combinatorial. Figure 1 illustrates the comprehensive nature of CISM (Everly and Mitchell, 1997).

As mentioned earlier, Bordow and Porritt (1979) demonstrated that multicomponent crisis intervention was, indeed, more effective than single unidimensional intervention. In a review contrasting single intervention approaches to multicomponent approaches to crisis intervention, Mitchell and Everly (in press) found a substantial body of literature supporting the efficacy of multicomponential intervention, while the results of single intervention crisis interventions were mixed. A similar finding was reached by Everly, Flannery, and Mitchell (1999) in an expanded review. A subsequent meta-analysis of empirical investigations into Critical Incident Stress Management revealed an extremely large and positive clinical effect (Everly, Flannery & Eyler, in press; Flannery, Everly & Eyler, 2000).

This is not to say that Critical Incident Stress Debriefings (CISD) have not shown their value. Mitchell and Everly (1997) reviewed the literature on this form of group crisis intervention and found it to be effective (see also Everly and Mitchell, 1999). In a series of meta-analyses, Everly and his colleagues have submitted the group crisis intervention of psychological, (Everly, Boyle & Lating, 1999) and specifically, CISD to meta-analyses (Everly and Boyle, 1999; Everly and Piaceutini, 1999) and found a powerful clinical effectiveness in evidence.

22

Table 1

CRITICAL INCIDENT STRESS MANAGEMENT (CISM):
The Core Components
(Adapted from: Everly and Mitchell, 1999)

	INTERVENTION	TIMING	ACTIVATION	GOAL	FORMAT
1.	Pre-crisis preparation	Pre-crisis phase	Crisis anticipation	Set expectations. Improve coping. Stress management.	Groups/ Organizations
2.	Demobilizations & staff consultation (rescuers)	Shift disengagement	Event driven.	To inform and consult, allow psychological decompression. Stress management.	Large groups/ Organizations
3.	Crisis Management Briefing (CMB) (civilians, schools, business)	Anytime post-crisis			
4.	Defusing	Post-crisis. (within 12 hours)	Usually symptom driven.	Symptom mitigation. Possible closure. Triage.	Small groups
5.	Critical Incident Stress Debriefing (CISD)	Post-crisis (1 - 10 days; 3-4 weeks mass disasters)	Usually symptom driven, can be event driven.	Facilitate psychological closure. Sx mitigation. Triage.	Small groups
6.	Individual crisis intervention 1:1	Anytime Anywhere	Symptom driven.	Symptom mitigation. Return to function, if possible. Referral, if needed.	Individuals
7.	Family CISM	Anytime	Either symptom driven or event driven.	Foster support & communications. Symptom mitigation. Closure, if possible. Referral, if needed.	Families/ Organizations
8.	Community and Organizational consultation				
9.	Pastoral Crisis Intervention	Anytime	Usually symptom driven	To mitigate a "crisis of faith" and use spiritual tools to assist in recovery.	Individuals. Families. Groups.
10.	Follow-up/Referral	Anytime	Usually symptom driven	Assess mental status. Access higher level of care, if needed.	Individual/ Family

[From: Everly, G. & Mitchell, J. (1999) Critical Incident Stress Management (CISM): A New Era and Standard of Care in Crisis Intervention. Ellicott City, MD: Chevron Publishing.]

REFERENCES

Bordow, S. & Porritt, D. (1979). An experimental evaluation of crisis intervention. *Social Science and Medicine, 13,* 251 - 256.

British Psychological Working (1990). *Psychological Aspects of Disaster.* Leicester: British Psychological Society.

Everly, G.S. & Boyle S. (1999). Critical Incident Stress Debriefing: A Meta-Analysis. *International Journal Emergency Mental Health, 1,* 165-168.

Everly G. S. ,Boyle, S., & Lating (1999). *Stress Medicine.*

Everly, G.S. & Flannery, R.B., & Eyler, V. (in press). Comprehensive crisis intervention: A statistical review. *Psychiatric Quarterly.*

Everly, G., Flannery, R. & Mitchell, J. (in press). CISM: A review of the literature. *Aggression and Violent Behavior: A Review Journal.*

Everly, G. S. & Mitchell, J. T. (1999). *Critical incident stress management (CISM): A new era and standard of care in crisis intervention (2nd Ed.).* Ellicott City, MD: Chevron Publishing Corporation.

Everly, G.S. & Piacentini, A. (1999, March). The effects of CISD on trauma symptoms: A meta-analysis. Paper presented to the APA-NIOSH Conference on Work, Stress and Health in a Global Economy, Baltimore.

Mitchell, J. T. (1983). When disaster strikes . . . The critical incident stress debriefing process. *Journal of Emergency Medical Services, 8 (1),* 36 - 39.

Mitchell, J. T. (1988). Development and functions of a critical incident stress debriefing team. *Journal of Emergency Medical Services, 13 (12),* 43 - 46.

Mitchell, J. T. & Everly, G. S. (1996). *Critical incident stress debriefing: An operations manual.* Ellicott City, MD: Chevron Publishing Corporation.

Mitchell, J. T. & Everly, G. S. (1997). Scientific evidence for CISM. *Journal of Emergency Medical Services, 22,* 87 - 93.

Mitchell, J. T. & Everly, G. S. (in press). CISM and CISD: Evolution, effects and outcomes. In B. Raphael & J. Wilson (Eds.). *Psychological Debriefing.*

Raphael, B. (1986). *When disaster strikes . . .* New York: Basic Books.

Figures 2 and 3 show how CISM services may be allocated across the crisis spectrum.

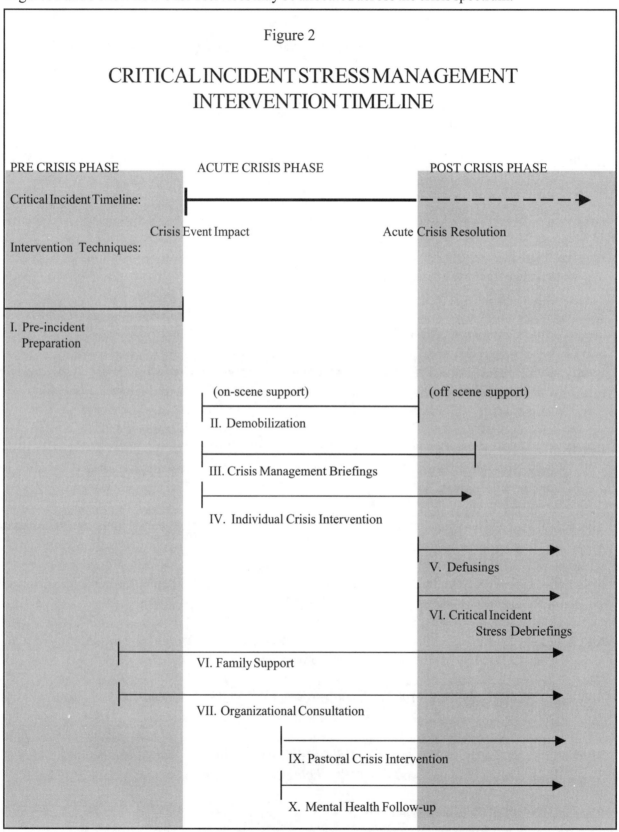

Figure 2

CRITICAL INCIDENT STRESS MANAGEMENT
INTERVENTION TIMELINE

(used with permission, Everly and Mitchell, 1999)

Figure 2 uses the concepts of precrisis, acute crisis and post crisis temporal phases to show the allocation of CISM services. Figure 3 uses an operations construct to demonstrate CISM allocation.

Figure 3

Critical Incident Stress Management

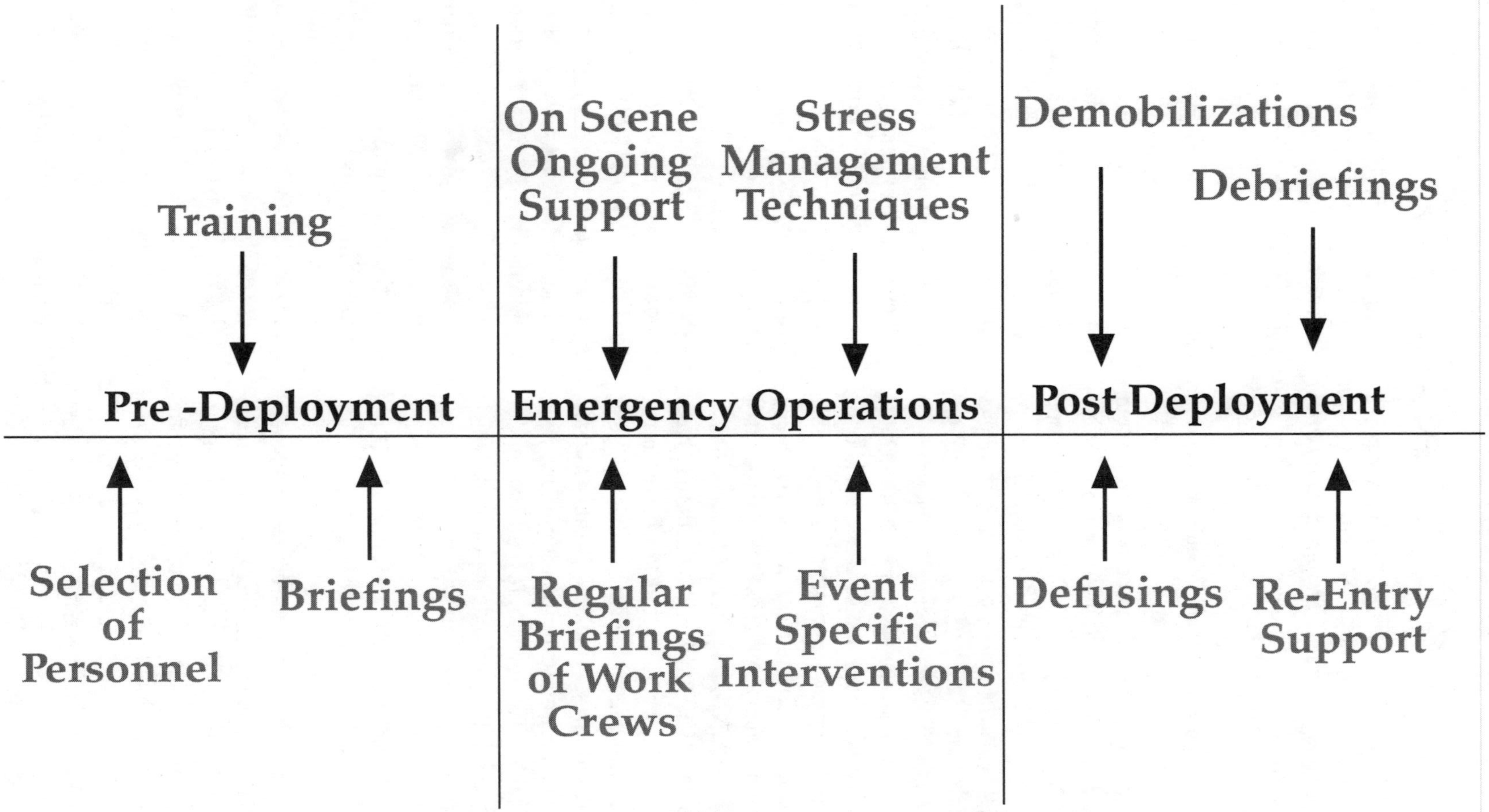

Dr. Atle Dyregrov
Bergen, Norway

Pre -Deployment

Training →

← Briefings

← Selection of Personnel

Emergency Operations

On Scene Ongoing Support →

Stress Management Techniques →

← Regular Briefings of Work Crews

← Event Specific Interventions

Post Deployment

Demobilizations →

Debriefings →

← Re-Entry Support

← Defusings

25

EMERGENCY MENTAL HEALTH: AN OVERVIEW

George S. Everly, Jr., Ph.D.

ABSTRACT: *As any field of endeavor evolves, as the field of emergency mental health is evolving, it becomes important to reflect upon historical milestones and define key terms. This paper is an effort to provide a brief overview of the field of emergency mental health and to take a glimpse at its future.* [*International Journal of Emergency Mental Health, 1999, 1, 3-7*]

KEY WORDS: Emergency Mental Health; crisis intervention; Critical Incident Stress Management

Emergency mental health may be thought of within the broadest context of crisis intervention, in effect it is crisis intervention, but much broader in scope than the 1960s and 1970s connotations of the term. Emergency mental health is the provision of mental health services with the goal(s) of 1) reducing the risk of acute and intense psychological crises or traumas, 2) stabilizing and reducing the immediate severity of a crisis or traumatic situation, and/or 3) facilitating recovery and restoration from a crisis or traumatic episode. Thus, such a view of emergency mental health actually embraces Caplan's notion of primary, secondary, and tertiary preventive mental health (Caplan, 1961, 1964), although the emphasis is placed upon the second formulation in the current application. Emergency mental health is practiced at the individual service level, the program development level, and even the community, state, and national levels. But is there really a need for such services? Is there a need for programs which provide urgent psychological support?

The Need for Emergency Mental Health Services

A crisis is usually defined as a condition wherein an individual's sense of psychological homeostasis is disrupted by some adverse event, or stressor, and most importantly, the usual coping mechanisms used by the individual in the past to reestablish

homeostasis are now proving ineffective (Caplan, 1961, 1964). The failure of one's usual coping strategies such as problem-solving and various ego defense mechanisms now leaves the individual in an ego-dystonic state of perceived inefficacy, vulnerability, and dysphoria. But how critical is this a threat to public health? Is there a need for programs which provide urgent psychological support?

Crises may certainly run the spectrum from mild situational crises to the extreme traumatic events as delineated by the DSM-IV (APA, 1994). Consider the following:

- 90% of United States citizens will be exposed to a traumatic event during their lifetime (Breslau, et al., 1998);
- The conditional risk of posttraumatic stress disorder (PTSD) was found to be 13% for females and 6% for males (Breslau, et al., 1998);
- Suicide rates have been seen to increase as much as almost 63% in the first year after an earthquake; increase by 31% in the first 2 years after a hurricane; and increase by almost 14% four years after a flood (Krug, et al., 1998);
- U. S. Citizens 12 years of age or older experienced 37 million crimes in 1996 (Bureau of Justice Statistics, 1997a);
- Approximately one million persons each year become victims of violent crimes while at work (Bachman, 1994);
- In 1994, U.S. hospital emergency rooms treated approximately 1.4 million individuals for

George S. Everly, Jr., Ph.D., Loyola College in Maryland and The Johns Hopkins University. Address correspondence concerning this article to: George S. Everly, Jr., Ph.D., 702 Severnside Ave., Severna Park, MD, 21146

injuries resulting from interpersonal violence (Bureau of Justice Statistics, 1997b);

- In 1997 there were 304 acts of international terrorism, one-third directed at United States targets.

- In a sample of urban United States firefighters, was discovered that almost 32% were assessed with symptoms consistent with a diagnosis of posttraumatic stress disorder (Beaton, Murphy, & Corneil, 1996).

Clearly, the aforementioned statistics argue that stressors and traumatic events are prevalent to such a degree so as to warrant serious attention from the mental health community. Emergency mental health responsiveness should be fostered so as to respond to this serous public health threat.

Emergency Mental Health: Crisis Intervention vs. Traditional Psychotherapy

As more and more mental health professionals are dispatched to perform acute disaster-related emergency mental health functions, it becomes ever more clear that to function effectively in emergency mental health, specialized training is requisite. Operationally stated, effective emergency mental health intervention represents an exercise in crisis intervention, not traditional psychotherapy. Koss and Shiang (1994) concluded that a substantial number of mental health professionals are providing some form of brief psychological intervention without having formal training to do so. This certainly raises

Table 1: Crisis Intervention vs. Psychotherapy

	Crisis Intervention	Psychotherapy
Context	Prevention.	Reparation.
Timing	Immediate, close temporal relationship to stressor or acute decompensation.	Delayed, distant from stressor or acute decompensation.
Location	Close proximity to stressor or acute decompensation. Anywhere needed.	Safe, secure environment.
Duration	1 to 3 contacts, typically.	As long as needed/desired.
Provider's Role	Active, directive.	Guiding, collaborative, consultative.
Strategic Foci	Conscious processes and environmental stressors/factors.	Conscious and unconscious sources of pathogenesis.
Temporal Focus	Here and now.	Present and past.
Patient Expectation	Directive, Sx reduction. Reduction of impairment. Directive support.	Symptom reduction, reduction of impairment, personal growth. Guidance and collaboration.
Goals	Stabilize, reduce impairment, return to function, or move to next level of care.	Symptom reduction, reduction of impairment, correction of pathogenesis, personal growth. Personal reconstruction.

SOURCES: Aguilera, et al. (1970); Artiss (1963); Everly & Mitchell (1998); Koss & Shiang, (1994); Salmon (1919); Sandoval (1985); Slaikeu (1990); Spiegel & Classen (1995); Wilkinson & Vera (1985).

serous ethical and legal concerns. Koss and Shiang (1994) point out that it raises outcome research issues as well. They note, "The systematic training of clinicians is a requirement for any outcome research that attempts to draw conclusions about effectiveness... (p. 676)." These authors conclude that increased levels of intervention training: 1) enhance intervention outcome, 2) lower interventionist attrition, 3) decrease relapse, and 4) improve the technical aspects of the intervention process itself.

Crisis intervention skills represent a specialized domain of therapeutic intervention. Admittedly, with the advent of terms such as "crisis therapy" and "brief psychotherapy" lines of distinction become more points on continua rather than stark categorical separations. As a result, Table 1 below attempts to explicitly address the difference between crisis intervention as an emergency mental health process vs. traditional psychotherapy.

Emergency Mental Health:
A Historical Review

The notion of providing acute psychological support to those individuals in acute distress is certainly not a new concept, nor is it the exclusive domain of one professional group, nor sector of society. Listed below are some of the important milestones in the emergency mental health field.

Perhaps the earliest formalized efforts to provide emergency psychological support in the United States were initiated at the turn of the twentieth century in the form of the National Save-A-Life League. This organization was founded in several large urban centers as an effort in suicide prevention.

World War I, however, yielded the first empirical observations that the provision of early psychological support could actually reduce psychiatric morbidity in the wake of extreme traumatic stressors (Salmon, 1919).

During World War II even more was learned about intervention with acute traumatic crises. Artiss (1963) identified the concepts of immediacy, proximity, and expectancy as key functional elements in effective crisis intervention.

Also during World War II Erich Lindemann (1944) explored the notion that swift psychological intervention and social support might facilitate constructive resolution of the grief process. His observations came in the wake of the 1943 Coconut Grove fire in which nearly 500 people died. For many, Lindemann's work marked the beginning of the "modern age" of crisis intervention.

In the late 1950s suicide prevention centers began to proliferate in the United States. Now, however, they represent true innovations in emergency mental health delivery: the use of telephone "hotlines," 24-hour availability, and the use of paraprofessional crisis counselors (Shneidman, 1967).

The 1960s and 1970s saw Gerald Caplan's (1961, 1964) concepts of preventive psychiatry operationalized with the creation of a system of community mental health centers as initiated by President John F. Kennedy. During this time the first research data began to emerge indicating that crisis intervention tactics could, indeed, be an effective mental health intervention by preventing psychiatric rehospitalization and reducing psychiatric disabilities (Decker and Stubblebine, 1972; Langsley, Machotka, & Flomenhaft, 1971; Parad & Parad, 1968).

In 1980, posttraumatic stress disorder (PTSD) was officially recognized as a psychiatric disorder within the Diagnostic and Statistical Manual of Mental disorders Third Edition (APA, 1980). Such nosological recognition was important because it provided an "official" nomenclature for the distress associated with crises and traumatic events, thus making related research and clinical activities more "legitimate."

The year 1982 engenders for many images of individuals being pulled from the icy Potomac River in Washington, D.C. as Air Florida 90 crash survivors were rescued. This mass disaster engendered a serious look at the stress reactions of emergency service/rescue personnel in the wake of traumatic events. It was also the first time that the Critical Incident Stress Debriefing (CISD) method for group crisis intervention was used in a mass disaster setting, even though it was formulated eight years earlier.

The year 1986 will be remembered as the beginning of the era of "violence in the workplace" as 13 postal workers were killed by a co-worker on the job in Oklahoma.

In response to growing recognition of the vulnerability of emergency services professionals (fire suppression, law enforcement, rescue, emergency medicine), the International Critical Incident Stress Foundation (ICISF) formalized an international network of over 350 crisis response teams using a sophisticated multicomponent crisis intervention system referred to as Critical Incident Stress Management (CISM; Everly and Mitchell, 1997). The ICISF gained United Nations affiliation in 1997.

In 1992, the American Red Cross initiated efforts to create a national disaster mental health network, later developing specialized training in aviation disasters.

In 1994, the Diagnostic and Statistical Manual of Mental Disorders, Fourth Edition (APA, 1994) added another diagnostic category to reflect the effects of crisis and trauma exposure. This new diagnosis was "acute stress disorder."

The year 1995 underscored the vulnerability of the United States to terrorism as the Federal Building was bombed in Oklahoma City. It also emphasized a need for crisis intervention services for victims, their families, as well as rescue personnel.

In 1996 the TWA 800 mass air disaster off Long Island, New York once again demonstrated the need for crisis services for the families of victims, as well as, rescue personnel.

The Occupational Safety and Health Administration (OSHA) began issuing recommendations on preventing violence and trauma in the workplace. OSHA recommended that the healthcare industry, social service agencies, and late-night retail establishments provide employees with violence prevention and crisis intervention programs (OSHA, 1996, 1998).

Finally in 1997, Vice-president of the United States Al Gore issued the Gore Commission Report on aviation safety and security. In that report, crisis intervention programs were recommended. Also, in 1997 the United States Air Force mandated that all U.S. Air Force bases would have critical incident stress response teams to serve the emergency mental health needs of those communities.

Thus, crisis intervention can be seen to have evolved significantly since the turn of the twentieth century with the development of increased recognition of the epidemic-like proportions of crisis/trauma related psychological problems, as well as the development of sophisticated multicomponent crisis intervention systems sometimes referred to as Critical Incident Stress Management (CISM) programs (Everly and Mitchell, 1997). For example, the Assaulted Staff Action Program (ASAP) is designed to attend to the crisis oriented psychological needs of healthcare, educational, and related service personnel (Flannery, 1998). Theoretically grounded and empirically validated, the ASAP program stands as a prototype for the development of multicomponent crisis intervention and violence prevention systems for the future.

Summary

In sum, while the field of emergency mental health has firm roots dating back nearly a century, it must be viewed as a field which is still emerging, still evolving. The renaissance of attention to psychological crises has spawned exciting new research, new program development, and entirely new intervention systems, such as CISM, and the Assaulted Staff Action Program (ASAP, Flannery, 1998). New research is showing that crisis intervention programs are effective and cost efficient (see Everly & Mitchell, 1997; Everly, Boyle, & Lating, 1999; Everly, Flannery, & Mitchell, 1999). The human resource is the most valuable resource that any organization possesses. Emergency mental health programs protect and enhance that most valuable of all resources, the human resource.

References

Aguilera, D. C., Messick, J., & Farrel, M. (1970). *Crisis Intervention.* St. Louis: Mosby.

American Psychiatric Association. (1980). *Diagnostic and Statistical Manual of Mental Disorders: Third Edition.* Washington, DC: Author.

American Psychiatric Association. (1994). *Diagnostic and Statistical Manual of Mental Disorders, Fourth Edition.* Washington DC: Author.

American Psychiatric Association. (1994). *Diagnostic and Statistical Manual of Mental Disorders, Fourth Edition.* Washington DC: APA Press.

Artiss, K. L. (1963). Human behavior under stress. *Military Medicine, 128,* 1011-1015.

Bachman, R. (1994, July 6). Violence and theft in the workplace. Crime Data Brief: National Crime Victimization survey. Washington DC: US Department of Justice.

Beaton, R., Murphy, S. & Corneil, W. (1996, Sept.) Prevalence of posttraumatic stress disorder symptomatology in professional urban firefighters in two countries. Paper presented at the International Congress of Occupational Health, Stockholm, Sweden.

Breslau, N., Kessler, R., Chilcoat, H., Schultz, L., Davis, G., & Andreski, P. (1998). Trauma and posttraumatic stress disorder in the community. *Archives of General Psychiatry, 55,* 626-623.

Bureau of Justice Statistics (1997a). *National Crime Victimization Survey.* Washington DC: US Department of Justice.

Bureau of Justice Statistics (1997b). *Violence-Related Injuries Treated in Hospital Emergency Departments.* Washington DC: U.S. Department of Justice.

Caplan, G. (1961). *An Approach to Community Mental Health.* NY: Grune and Stratton.

Caplan, G. (1964). *Principles of Preventive Psychiatry.* NY: Basic Books.

Decker, B., & Stubblebine, J. (1972). Crisis intervention and the prevention of psychiatric disability: A follow-up study. *American Journal of Psychiatry, 129,* 725-729.

Everly, G.S., Boyle. & Lating, J. (1999). The effectiveness of psychological debriefings in vicarious trauma: A meta-analysis. *Stress Medicine.*

Everly, G.S., Flannery, R.B. & Mitchell, J.T. (1999). Critical Incident Stress Management: A review of literature. *Aggression and Violent Behavior: A Review Journal.*

Everly, G.S. & Mitchell, J.T. (1998). *Assisting Individuals in Crisis: A Workbook.* Ellicott City, MD: ICISF.

Everly, G. S. & Mitchell, J.T. (1997). *Critical Incident Stress Management (CISM): A New Era and Standard of Care in Crisis Intervention.* Ellicott City, MD: Chevron Publishing.

Flannery, R.B. (1998). *The Assaulted Staff Action Program: Coping with the Psychological Aftermath of Violence.* Ellicott City, MD: Chevron Publishing.

Gore, A. (1997). *White House Commission Report on Aviation Safety and Security.* Washington DC: The White House.

Koss, M. & Shiang, J. (1994). Research on brief psychotherapy. In A. Bergin and S. Garfield (Eds). *Handbook of Psychotherapy and Behavior Change* (pp. 664-700). NY: John Wiley.

Krug, E.G., Kresnow, M., Peddicord, J., Dahlberg, L., Powell, K., Crosby, A., & Annest, J. (1998). Suicide after natural disasters. *New England Journal of Medicine, 338,* 373-378.

Langsley, D., Machotka, P., & Flomenhaft, K., (1971). Avoiding mental health admission: A follow-up. *American Journal of Psychiatry, 127,* 1391-1394.

Lindemann, E. (1944). Symptomatology and management of acute grief. *American Journal of Psychiatry, 101,* 141-148.

OSHA. (1996). *Guidelines for Preventing Workplace Violence for Healthcare and Social Service Workers*
(OSHA) 3148-1996. Washington DC: US Department of Labor. OSHA. (1998). *Recommendations for Workplace Violence Prevention Programs in Late-Night Retail Establishments.*
(OSHA) 3153-1998. Washington DC: US Department of Labor.

Parad, L. & Parad, H. (1968). A study of crisis-oriented planned short-term treatment: Part II. *Social Casework, 49*, 418-426.

Salmon, T.W. (1919). War neuroses and their lesson. *New York Medical Journal., 59*, 993-994.

Sandoval, J. (1985). Crisis counseling: Conceptualizations and general principles. *School Psychology Review 14*, 257 - 265.

Shneidman, E. (Ed.) (1967). *Essays in Self-Destruction.* NY: Science House.

Slaikeu, K. A. (1990). *Crisis Intervention* (2nd). Boston: Allyn and Bacon.

Spiegel, D. & Classen, C. (1995). Acute Stress Disorder. In G. Gabbard, (Ed.). *Treatments of Psychiatric Disorders, Second Edition* (pp. 1521-1536). Washington, DC: American Psychiatric Press.

Wilkinson, C. B. & Vera, E. (1985). Management and treatment of disaster victims. *Psychiatric Annals, 15*, 174-184.

Notes

Section Two

STRESS

HUMAN STRESS: BASIC TERMS AND CONDITIONS

Stressor - A stimulus that causes, evokes, or is otherwise strongly associated with the stress response.

Stress Response - Nonspecific response of the body to any demand. Stress consists of a well known combination of neurologic, neuroendocrine, and endocrine arousal response mechanisms that can affect and alter every organ and function of the human body. Stress accelerates the aging process as we know it. Dr. Hans Selye once said stress is the sum total of "wear and tear" on the body. Stress = Arousal.

Target Organs - The part of the body, or mind, that is the "target" of the stress response and which develops signs and symptoms of overarousal.

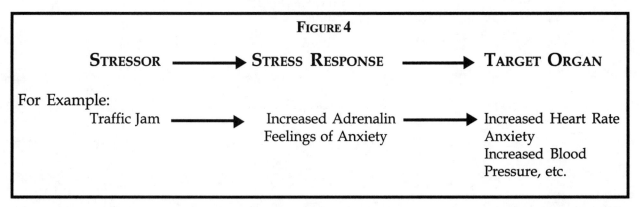

Cumulative Stress - Stress arousal that slowly builds up over time, sometimes, leading to a condition of "burnout." Cumulative stress erodes coping mechanisms.

Eustress - The term applied to stress as a positive motivating force which may lead to increased health and performance.

Distress - The term applied to stress as a negative dysfunctional force that may lead to disease and the erosion of health.

Burnout - A state of mental and physical exhaustion (see also cumulative stress). The burnout process has 3 phases:

     I   Stress Arousal Phase which may include:
        a. anxiety
        b. panic
        c. difficulty concentrating
        d. feeling out of control or overwhelmed
        e. stress related physical symptoms such as tachycardia, arrhythmias, gastrointestinal distress, rashes, acute elevation in blood pressure, muscle tension syndromes/spasms, headaches, etc.

II Energy Conservation Phase which consists of:
   a. procrastination
   b. lateness
   c. absenteeism
   d. increased coffee, tea, soda, tobacco consumption
   e. withdrawal, avoidance

III Exhaustion Phase which may include:
   a. feelings of hopelessness and/or helplessness
   b. fully developed depression
   c. serious consideration of changing job status
   d. serious consideration of changing personal living situation
   e. desire to withdraw, take a "geographic cure"
   f. contemplation of self-destruction actions
   g. substance abuse

CUMULATIVE STRESS REACTION

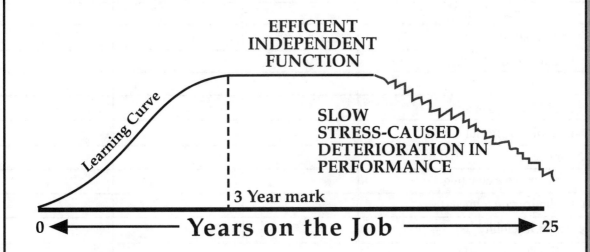

IDENTIFYING YOUR MOST COMMON
SYMPTOMS OF DISTRESS

Most people know when they are experiencing excessive levels of stress arousal. The manner in which we are alerted to such a condition of distress may be through the development of symptoms of excessive stress. Listed below are numerous potentially stress-related symptoms that people experience. Read through the list and check your most common symptoms of distress putting a check in the column indicating how often you experience each.

"When I am under a great deal of stress, I experience:"			
	Seldom	**Sometimes**	**Often**
1. Headaches			
2. Irregular heart beat			
3. Muscle spasms			
4. Gastrointestinal problems			
5. Vertigo			
6. High blood pressure			
7. Low blood pressure			
8. Fatigue			
9. Difficulty concentrating			
10. Feeling overwhelmed			
11. Anger, irritability			
12. Difficulty falling asleep or staying asleep			
13. Sadness/depression			
14. Increased appetite			
15. Decreased appetite			
16. Rashes or hives			
17. Feelings of helplessness or hopelessness			
18. Apathy			
19. Increased use of alcohol and/or tobacco			
20. Cynicism, negativism			

Section Three

STRESS MANAGEMENT

STRESS MANAGEMENT

Stress Management - The term applied to the conscious effort to better control, mitigate, or interact with the stress in one's life.

Stress Management techniques may be divided into 4 major categories:

I. Techniques to avoid or reduce exposure to stressors
    a. Problem solving
    b. Time management
    c. Nutritional techniques
    d. Avoiding known stressors

II. Techniques to reappraise or reinterpret stressors
    a. Cognitive reframing
    b. Psychotherapy

III. Techniques to reduce stress arousal
    a. Proper sleep patterns
    b. Relaxation response training (e.g., meditation, imagery, biofeedback, etc.)
    c. Prescription anxiolytic medications

IV. Techniques to ventilate the stress arousal
    a. Physical exercise
    b. Catharsis

There is no one best relaxation technique; nor is there one best stress management technique. Stress management is a very personal process. The key to a successful stress management program is consistency. To be most effective stress management should become part of one's life-style, not just a technique to be used if one gets "stressed out." Valuable resource guides for stress management are:

D. Girdano, G. Everly, Jr. and D. Dusek (2001) *Controlling Stress and Tension: A Holistic Approach*. 6th Edition. Englewood Cliffs, NJ: Prentice-Hall.

J. Mitchell and G. Bray (1990). *Emergency Services Stress*. Englewood Cliffs, NJ: Brady.

For more technical background on stress and stress management see
G. Everly, Jr. (1989). *A Clinical Guide to the Treatment of the Human Stress Response*. NY: Plenum Press.

Sympathomimetics - A form of stimulant which increases the level of stress arousal.
Common sources of sympathomimetics include:
      a. Coffee
      b. Tea
      c. Sodas (which contain caffeine)
      d. Tobacco products
      e. Diet pills

A useful stress management concept is to reduce or eliminate the use of such substances during periods of increased work-related or personal distress.

Relaxation Response - A hypometabolic response known to be the antithesis of stress arousal. The term, first coined by cardiologist Herbert Benson in his 1974 book, *The Relaxation Response*, was applied to the response engendered through the practice of various relaxation techniques such as mantra meditation, imagery, progressive muscle relaxation, etc. To be effective as a stress management tool and to facilitate the recovery from cumulative or trauma stress, the relaxation response should be practiced 15-20 minutes each day.

HOW DO YOU COPE WITH STRESS?

Directions: There are many ways to cope with the stress in your life. Some coping techniques are more effective than others. The purpose of this checklist is to help you assess how effectively you cope with the stress. Upon completing this checklist, you will have identified many of the ways you choose to cope with stress, while at the same time, through a point system, ascertain the relative desirability of the coping techniques that you now employ. This is a health education survey, not a clinical assessment instrument. Its sole purpose is to inform you of how you cope with the stress in your life.

In order to complete the checklist, simply follow the instructions given for each of the 14 items listed below. When you have completed all of the 14 items, place your total score in the space provided.

_10_ 1. Give yourself 10 points if you feel that you have a supportive family.

_10_ 2. Give yourself 10 points if you actively pursue a hobby.

_____ 3. Give yourself 10 points if you belong to some social or activity group that meets at least once a month (other than your family).

_15_ 4. Give yourself 15 points if you are within five pounds of your "ideal" bodyweight, considering your height and bone structure.

_____ 5. Give yourself 15 points if you practice some form of "deep relaxation" at least three times a week. Deep relaxation exercises include meditation, imagery, yoga, etc.

_____ 6. Give yourself 5 points for each time you exercise 30 minutes or longer during the course of an average week.

_5_ 7. Give yourself 5 points for each nutritionally balanced and wholesome meal you consume during the course of an average day.

_10_ 8. Give yourself 10 points for each time you do something that you really enjoy, "just for yourself," during the course of an average week.

_10_ 9. Give yourself 10 points if you have some place in your home that you can go to in order to relax and/or be by yourself.

_____ 10. Give yourself 10 points if you practice time management techniques in your daily life.

_____ 11. Subtract 10 points for each pack of cigarettes you smoke during the course of an average day.

_-15_ 12. Subtract 5 points for each evening during the course of an average week that you take any form of medication or chemical substance (including alcohol) to help you sleep.

_-30_ 13. Subtract 10 points for each day during the course of an average week that you consume any form of medication or chemical substance (including alcohol) to reduce your anxiety or just calm you down.

_____ 14. Subtract 5 points for each evening during the course of an average week that you bring work home; work that was meant to be done at your place of employment.

_95_ **TOTAL SCORE**

Now that you've calculated your score, consider that the higher your score, the greater your health-promoting coping practices. A "perfect" score would be around 115. Scores in the 50-60 range are probably adequate to cope with most common sources of stress.

Also keep in mind that items 1-10 represent adaptive health-promoting coping strategies, and items 11-14 represent maladaptive, health-deteriorating coping strategies. These maladaptive strategies are self-sustaining because they do provide at least some temporary relief from stress. In the long run, however, their utilization serves to erode one's health. Ideally, health-promoting coping strategies (items 1-10) are the best to integrate into your lifestyle and will ultimately prove to be an effective preventive program against excessive stress.

This exercise was developed by Dr. George S. Everly, Jr. through a grant provided by the U.S.H.E.W.

AN "INSTANT" RELAXATION EXERCISE

This exercise is adapted from the G.S. Everly, Jr. (1989) *A Clinical Guide to the Treatment of the Human Stress Response*. NY: Plenum Press.

At times we find ourselves overexcited, angry, or just needing to calm down. This simple breathing exercise may be a valuable tool for reducing excessive arousal quickly and effectively during upsetting moments, in effect, a quick way to "calm down" in the face of a stressful situation.

The basic mechanism for stress reduction in this exercise involves deep breathing. The procedure is as follows:

STEP 1 - Assume a comfortable position. Rest your left hand (palm down) on top of your navel. Now place your right hand so that it comfortably rests on your left. Your eyes should remain open.

STEP 2 - Imagine a hollow bottle, or pouch, lying internally beneath the point at which your hands are resting. Begin to inhale, imagine that the air is entering through your nose and descending to fill that internal pouch. Your hands will rise as you fill the pouch with air. As you continue to inhale, imagine the pouch being filled to the top. Your rib cage and upper chest will continue the wavelike rise that was begun at your navel. The total length of your inhalation should be 3 seconds for the first week or so, then lengthen to 4 to 5 seconds as your progress in skill development.

STEP 3 - Slowly begin to exhale - to empty the pouch. As you do, repeat to yourself the phrase "My body is calm." As you exhale, you will feel your raised abdomen and chest recede.

Repeat this exercise two times in succession. Then continue to breathe normally for 5 to 10 successive breath cycles, but be sure to emphasize the expiration of each breath as the point of relaxation. Then you may repeat the entire process again - 2 deep breaths followed by 5 to 10 normal breaths during which you concentrate on releasing any stored tension on the expiration. Should you begin to feel light-headed or should you experience any discomfort, stop at that point. You may wish to shorten the length of the inhalation to avoid light-headedness.

After about one week of practicing, omit STEP 1, start with STEP 2. If you have any health concerns, consult your physician prior to using this exercise. <u>Never</u> use this exercise while driving.

<u>*Notes*</u>

Section Four

TRAUMATIC STRESS

TRAUMATIC STRESS

Trauma - Any event outside the usual realm of human experience that is markedly distressing (e.g., evokes reactions of intense fear, helplessness, horror, etc.) Such traumatic stressors usually involve the perceived threat to one's physical integrity or to the physical integrity of someone in close proximity.

Post-Traumatic Stress - Very intense arousal subsequent to a traumatic stressor (trauma). Traumatic stress overwhelms coping mechanisms leaving individuals out of control and feeling helpless.

Post-Traumatic Stress Disorder (PTSD) - The term applied as the official diagnosis of a post-traumatic stress syndrome that is characterized by symptoms of:
   a. excessive excitability and arousal,
   b. numbing withdrawal, and avoidance, and
   c. repetitive, intrusive memories or recollections of the trauma and/or events related to the trauma,
   d. duration of at least 1 month,
   e. causing significant distress/dysfunction

Psychotraumatology - The term applied to the study of psychological trauma, more specifically, the factors antecedent to, concomitant with, and subsequent to psychological traumatization.

See G. Everly Jr. and J.M. Lating (Eds.) (1995) *Psychotraumatology: Key papers and Core Concepts in Post-Traumatic Stress*. NY: Plenum.

Trauma Membrane - Concept developed by J. Lindy that argues that subsequent to insulates them from continued intrusion or over-stimulation; however, it also insulates them from efforts by others to assist in their recovery. The membrane "thickens" with time; therefore early intervention after trauma or disaster is highly recommended.

CRITICAL INCIDENT STRESS REACTION

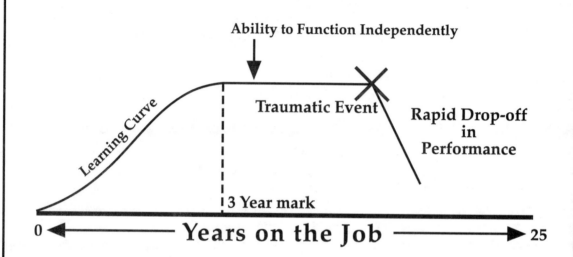

POTENTIALLY TRAUMATIZING EVENTS	
INDIVIDUAL	**COMMUNITY**
1. Automobile accident	1. Earthquake
2. Sexual assault/abuse	2. Hurricane
3. Any life threatening experience	3. Fires
4. Robbery	4. Flood
5. Serious physical injury/abuse	5. Large scale environmental pollution
6. Perception of serious threat to self or significant other	6. Multiple injury/fatality accidents
7. Psychological abuse	7. Terrorism
8. Severe injury/death of one's own child	8. Child related traumatic events
9. Suicide of family member or co-worker	9. Homicides in the community
10. Homicide	10. High publicity crimes of violence or sex
11. Line of duty injury or death among law enforcement or other first responders	11. Community wide disasters
12. Multiple homicides within a community	
13. Injury or death to a child	
14. Observing any of the individual or community trauma listed above	

COMMON SIGNS AND SYMPTOMS
OF EXCESSIVE STRESS

COGNITIVE

Confusion in thinking
Difficulty making decisions
Disorientation

PHYSICAL

Excessive sweating
Dizzy spells
Increased heart rate
Elevated blood pressure
Rapid breathing

EMOTIONAL

Emotional shock
Anger
Grief
Depression
Feeling overwhelmed
Hopelessness / helplessness

BEHAVIORAL

Changes in ordinary behavior patterns
Changes in eating
Decreased personal hygiene
Withdrawal from others
Prolonged silences

EARLY WARNINGS OF POSSIBLE PTSD

- Dissociation

- Traumatic dreams

- Memory disturbances

- Persistent intrusive recollections of the trauma

- Self-medication (e.g., alcohol abuse)

- Anger, irritability, hostility which is difficult to control

- Persistent depression, withdrawal

- A "dazed" or "numb" appearance

- Panic attacks

- Phobia formation

POTENTIAL POST-TRAUMATIC STRESS SYNDROMES

- Post-Traumatic Stress Disorder (PTSD)

- Complex partial seizures

- Depression

- Self-medicating, substance abuse

- Personality disorders (Borderline, Antisocial, Multiple Personality, Schizotypal)

- Erratic work-related behavior

- Memory dysfunction without traumatic amnesia

- Amnesiac syndromes regarding traumatization

TRAUMATIC STRESS AWARENESS

Remember the last significant critical incident to which you were exposed. Using the list below, indicate which symptoms you experienced, if any, and how long they persisted.

1. Nightmares (more than once/week)   _____

2. Intrusive memories (more than once/day)   _____

3. Irritability   _____

4. Difficulty concentrating   _____

5. Anger/hostility   _____

6. Fear and/or avoidance of similar situations   _____

7. Avoidance of people or things that remind
    you of the critical incident   _____

8. Stress-related physical complaints   _____

9. Flashbacks   _____

10. Withdrawal from usual activities   _____

11. Feeling "numb" or detached   _____

12. Depressed mood   _____

13. Feeling guilty   _____

14. Feeling anxious   _____

15. Feeling as though the world no longer
    "makes sense"   _____

16. Questioning religious values   _____

17. Hypervigilance   _____

18. Exaggerated startle response   _____

19. Difficulty sleeping   _____

20. Difficulty remembering the critical incident _____

21. Feeling estranged from your body   _____

22. Feeling estranged from your surroundings   _____

Section Five

DEMOBILIZATIONS

DEMOBILIZATION

Definition: Quick informational and rest session applied when operations units have been released from service at a major incident that requires over 100 personnel. It serves a secondary function as a screening opportunity to assure that individuals who may need assistance are identified after the traumatic event.

Length of time: 10 minute information section from CISM team member
20 minutes for food and rest

Best applied: Immediately after work teams have been released from the major incident and before personnel return to normal duties.

Target: Teams of workers. Engine or truck companies, ambulance units, perimeter control teams, entry teams, search teams, dog teams, squads, special units, etc. Each team receives its own demobilization session.

Provided By: Trained Critical Incident Stress Team members only.

Location of Demobilization: Two large rooms. One to provide the information sessions in small work groups, the other to provide the food and rest. The facility should be near enough to the scene to be convenient to transfer personnel there when they have been released from the incident.

Goals:
1. Assess well-being of personnel after major incident
2. Mitigate impact of event
3. Provide stress management information to personnel
4. Provide an opportunity for rest and food before returning to routine duties
5. Assess need for debriefing and other services

Process:
1. Establish an appropriate demobilization center
2. Check in units as they arrive
3. Keep work teams together for demobilization
4. Assign a CIS trained team member to provide information to the group
5. Limit the information section to ten minutes
6. Provide twenty minutes to rest and eat
7. Let participants know if a debriefing is planned
8. Provide a handout on stress survival suggestions

58

Contraindications:

1. Not for routine events
2. Not for small sized events.
3 Not a substitute for debriefing
4. Not for line of duty death (use CISD instead)

Demobilizations are very rare. They are reserved for large scale incidents such as disasters.

A defusing can substitute for a demobilization if the size of the incident allows for the lengthier defusing process and if the personnel are not too weary. If they are too tired, it is better to just give them the shorter demobilization process and let the personnel get rest.

No one except the team member presenting in the demobilization has to speak. No questions are asked. If someone wants to speak, he may. Work groups (police, fire, EMS, etc.) are **not** mixed.

Demobilization Components:

1. Check in by unit
2. CISM team member gives 10-minute talk on stress survival skills:
   a) describe typical reactions
   b) list signs and symptoms
   c) provide brief suggestions on surviving stress reactions
   d) invite anyone who wants to make a statement or ask questions to do so
3. In a separate room provide food and rest for twenty minutes until personnel are restored to routine functions.
4. Command or supervisory person makes announcements and personnel are restored to normal duties.

During any demobilization the following topics are usually covered:

- An introduction of the speaker

- A review of the demobilization process. A statement that the speaker is only going to take ten minutes to provide some important information that may prevent stress or help personnel to cope with it faster and easier. A prolonged mission (e.g., a military operation) may require a longer information segment (up to 30 minutes)

- A statement that some may already have stress symptoms, some may develop them later, and some may escape them altogether

- Assurance that stress symptoms are normal under the circumstances

- A warning that stress symptoms could become dangerous or disruptive to the personnel if they are ignored

- Descriptions of common cognitive, physical, emotional and behavioral signs and symptoms of stress

- Specific advice on eating, resting, avoiding alcohol, and drugs, conversing with loved ones, coping with the media, and other helpful hints to recover from stress

- An announcement of debriefings to follow in a week or so after the demobilization

- A brief statement to encourage the participants to ask questions or to make any comments they might wish

- A summary statement from the speaker

- Distribution of the handout material

KEY CONCEPTS
DEMOBILIZATION

- Reserve for large scale event

- A debriefing must follow within a few days to several weeks

- CISM team member must provide services

- Never provide it at the scene

- Does not require mental health professional

- One work team after another is processed until all of the personnel involved in the situation have been processed

- Once the demobilization is complete, personnel do not return to the incident. Instead they return to routine duties, or they go home if their duty time is complete

- Keep remarks very brief. Only provide the basic information necessary to hold the personnel together until more definitive work such as debriefing can be done

- Instruct personnel about interactions with loved ones at home who may be distressed by the incident

- Instruct personnel how to obtain help if they need it before the debriefing is provided

- Be available to personnel if they would like to discuss the incident privately

- Assure that command staff also receive support

- Provide low fat, low sugar, low salt foods that have complex carbohydrates in the food service area

- Avoid caffeine products in food service

- Allow commanders to announce the next steps for the personnel after the demobilization concludes the food and rest phase

- Be familiar with demobilization material in the *CISD: An Operations manual* ...

- Additional information may be found in the *CISD: An Operations Manual, 3rd edition,* (Mitchell and Everly, 2001)

Section Six

CRISIS
MANAGEMENT
BRIEFINGS
(CMB)

CRISIS MANAGEMENT BRIEFING
(CMB)

Definition: A large group crisis intervention technique. Designed for use with large groups of primary victims (up to 300 at a time). May be implemented with civilians after mass disasters, students after school-related incidents, employees after work-related crises, and even large military units.

Applications: Terrorism, mass disasters, community violence, school crises, work-place crises, military and naval crises.

Length of Time: 45 - 75 minutes

Goals:
1) Provide information
2) Rumor control
3) Reduce sense of chaos
4) Provide coping resources
5) Facilitate follow-up care
6) Engender increased cohesion and morale
7) Assess further needs of group
8) Restore personnel to adaptive functions

Process:
Step 1:   Assemble participants
Step 2: Provide facts regarding crisis
Step 3: Discuss and normalize common behavioral/psychological reactions
Step 4: Discuss personal and community stress management. Direct toward further resources

Innovations

CRISIS MANAGEMENT BRIEFINGS (CMB): LARGE GROUP CRISIS INTERVENTION IN RESPONSE TO TERRORISM, DISASTERS, AND VIOLENCE

George S. Everly, Jr., Ph.D.

ABSTRACT: *A single act of violence or terrorism can adversely affect thousands of people. Such acts will invariably engender a psychological morbidity that will far surpass any physical morbidity. Heretofore, efforts in primary and secondary prevention have focused largely upon the physical consequences of these incidents, rather than their psychological consequences. This paper describes a practical group psychological crisis intervention, the "crisis management briefing" (CMB), that may be used with large groups of individuals in the wake of terrorism, violence, disasters, and other crises. This intervention, which is one component of the Critical Incident Stress Management (CISM) crisis intervention system, is designed to mitigate the effects of these crises and requires anywhere from 45 to 75 minutes to implement. The CBM may be employed with groups ranging from 10 to 300 individuals at one time [International Journal of Emergency Mental Health, 2000, 2(1), 53-57].*

KEYWORDS: Crisis intervention; crisis management briefing; terrorism; violence; disasters; Critical Incident Stress Management (CISM); traumatic stress

There can be little doubt that disasters, violence, and acts of terrorism engender a large scale psychological morbidity. In fact, the explicit goal of any true act of terrorism is to create a condition of fear, uncertainty, demoralization, and helplessness, i.e., "terror." As Shreiber (1978) noted, the direct target or victims of the terrorist act are not the real targets, rather they are but the means to an end. In the cases of terrorism, mass disasters, and acts of violence, the "psychological casualties" will virtually always outnumber the "physical casualties." Any effective response to such crises simply must mandate psychological intervention, as well as physical crisis intervention.

George S. Everly, Jr., Ph.D., Loyola College in Maryland, The Johns Hopkins University, and Universidad de Flores. Address correspondence concerning this article to: Dr. George Everly, Jr., 702 Severnside Ave., Severna Park, MD 21146, USA.

As an example, the Defense Against Weapons of Mass Destruction Act of 1996 (Senators Nunn, Lugar, & Domenici) mandates the enhancement of domestic preparedness and response capabilities in the wake of attacks against the United States using weapons of mass destruction (WMD). Although a small component, provisions are made for psychological crisis intervention with both emergency responders and primary civilian victim populations. This paper describes a group psychological crisis intervention designed to mitigate the levels of felt crisis and traumatic stress in the wake of terrorism, mass disasters, violence, and other "large scale" crises. The intervention is referred to as the "crisis management briefing" (CMB) and is designed to be used with "large groups" of primary civilian victims which may range in size from 10 to 300 individuals at one time. The intervention is designed to be highly efficient, taking between 45 and 75 minutes to implement. The CMB may be implemented in schools, corporations, and community settings. The CMB is but one component of the comprehensive Critical Incident Stress Management (CISM) crisis intervention system.

A REVIEW OF CRITICAL INCIDENT STRESS MANAGEMENT (CISM)

Crises and disasters seem almost epidemic. The threat of mass terrorism has become an ever-increasing reality. Even the instant mass media coverage of these events may, for some, represent a source of vicarious traumatization. In consideration of these realities, the need for effective psychological crisis response capabilities becomes obvious. Crisis intervention programs are recommended and even mandated in a wide variety of community and occupational settings (Everly & Mitchell, 1999). Critical Incident Stress Management (CISM) represents a powerful, yet cost-effective approach to crisis response (Everly, Flannery, & Mitchell, 1999; Flannery, 1998; Everly & Mitchell, 1999; Everly & Boyle, 1999; Everly, Flannery, & Eyler, 2000).

What is CISM? CISM is a comprehensive, integrative, multicomponent crisis intervention system. CISM is considered comprehensive because it consists of multiple crisis intervention components which span both the temporal and functional spectra of a crisis. CISM interventions range from the pre-crisis phase, through the acute crisis phase, and into the post-crisis phase. CISM is also considered comprehensive in that it consists of interventions which may be applied to individuals, small functional groups, large groups, families, organizations, and even entire communities. The

core components of CISM are defined below and are summarized in TABLE 1.

1. Pre-crisis preparation. This includes stress management education, stress resistance, and crisis mitigation training for both individuals and organizations.
2. Disaster, terrorist, or other large scale incident interventions, including but not limited to: a) demobilizations for emergency response personnel, b) crisis management briefings (CMB) for school, corporate, and general civilian populations, c) "town meetings," and d) incident command staff advisement.
3. Defusing. This is a 3-phase, structured small group discussion provided within hours of a crisis for purposes of assessment, triaging, and acute symptom mitigation.
4. Critical Incident Stress Debriefing (CISD) refers to the "ICISF model" (Mitchell & Everly, 1996) 7-phase, structured group discussion, usually provided 1 to 10 days post crisis (3 to 4 weeks post disaster), and designed to mitigate acute symptoms, assess the need for follow-up, and if possible provide a sense of post-crisis psychological closure.
5. One-on-one crisis intervention/counseling or psychological support throughout the full range of the crisis spectrum (Everly & Mitchell, 1999).
6. a) Family crisis intervention, as well as, b) organizational consultation.
7. Follow-up and referral mechanisms for assessment and treatment, if necessary.

The effectiveness of CISM programs has been validated through thoughtful qualitative analyses (Everly & Mitchell, 1999; Everly, Flannery, & Mitchell, 1999; Miller, 1999; Dyregrov, 1997; Mitchell & Everly, in press), as well as through controlled investigations, and even meta-analyses (Everly, Boyle, & Lating, 1999; Everly & Boyle, 1999; Everly & Piacentini, 1999; Flannery, Penk,

Table 1

CRITICAL INCIDENT STRESS MANAGEMENT (CISM):
The Core Components

(Adapted from: Everly and Mitchell, 1999)

INTERVENTION	TIMING	ACTIVATION	GOAL	FORMAT
1. Pre-crisis preparation	Pre-crisis phase	Crisis anticipation	Set expectations. Improve coping. Stress management.	Groups/ Organizations
2. Demobilizations & staff consultation (rescuers)	Shift disengagement	Event driven.	To inform and consult, allow psychological decompression. Stress management.	Large groups/ Organizations
3. Crisis Management Briefing (CMB) (civilians, schools, business)	Anytime post-crisis			
4. Defusing	Post-crisis. (within 12 hours)	Usually symptom driven.	Symptom mitigation. Possible closure. Triage.	Small groups
5. Critical Incident Stress Debriefing (CISD)	Post-crisis (1 - 10 days; 3-4 weeks mass disasters)	Usually symptom driven, can be event driven.	Facilitate psychological closure. Sx mitigation. Triage.	Small groups
6. Individual crisis intervention 1:1	Anytime Anywhere	Symptom driven.	Symptom mitigation. Return to function, if possible. Referral, if needed.	Individuals
7. Family CISM	Anytime	Either symptom driven or event driven.	Foster support & communications. Symptom mitigation. Closure, if possible. Referral, if needed.	Families/ Organizations
8. Community and Organizational consultation				
9. Pastoral Crisis Intervention	Anytime	Usually symptom driven	To mitigate a "crisis of faith" and use spiritual tools to assist in recovery.	Individuals. Families. Groups.
10. Follow-up/Referral	Anytime	Usually symptom driven	Assess mental status. Access higher level of care, if needed.	Individual/ Family

[From: Everly, G. & Mitchell, J. (1999) Critical Incident Stress Management (CISM): A New Era and Standard of Care in Crisis Intervention. Ellicott City, MD: Chevron Publishing.]

67

& Corrigan, 1999; Everly, Flannery, & Eyler, 2000; Flannery, 1998). Although not all reviews support the effectiveness of psychological crisis intervention programs such as CISM (Rose & Bisson, 1998), close scrutiny of ineffective outcome reveals the lack of a standardized, multicomponent intervention program. The standardized and multicomponent nature of the CISM system serves to remedy this shortcoming.

CRISIS MANAGEMENT BRIEFINGS (CMB)

The "crisis management briefing" (CMB) is a practical four-phase group crisis intervention. It is designed to be highly efficient in that it requires from 45 to 75 minutes to conduct and may be used with "large" groups consisting of 10 to 300 individuals. While designed to be used with primary victim civilian populations in the wake of terrorism, mass disasters, violence, and other large-scale crises, it may have applicability in other settings with other populations, as well. As noted in TABLE 1, the CMB (component 2b on TABLE 1) is but one component within the comprehensive CISM system as described by Everly and Mitchell (1999; Mitchell & Everly, 1996). The CMB is designed to be used within a comprehensive CISM framework, and should not be used as a "stand-alone" intervention. It is anticipated that, depending upon the crisis event, there will be a need for CISD (component 4 on TABLE 1) and individual (1:1) crisis interventions (component 5) subsequent to the CMB. And, as always, arrangements should be made for follow-up assessment and referral for continued psychological care (component 7), if needed.

PHASE ONE: The first phase of the CMB consists of bringing together a group of individuals who have experienced a common crisis event. In response to a school crisis, for example, an assembly could be held in the auditorium.

Depending upon the number of students, one grade could be addressed at a time, or other divisions of the student body could be used. In response to a workplace crisis, a company meeting room could be used, or a room could be rented at a local hotel or commercial meeting facility. In response to mass disasters, large-scale violence, or terrorism, local school auditoriums could be used to address the civilian populations that would correspond to the respective school districts. Announcements to that effect could be made via radio, television, and internet sites. Obviously, the CMB would be repeated until all constituents have been addressed within the given circumscribed area/population. This act of assembly is the first step in reestablishing the sense of community that is so imperative to the recovery and rebuilding process (Ayalon, 1993).

PHASE TWO: Once the group has been assembled, the next intervention component is to have the most appropriate and credible sources/authorities explain the *facts* of the crisis event. In many instances, the choice of a respected and highly credible spokesperson assists in the development of the perceived credibility of the message and the belief that the actions and support will be effective. The ethos of the spokesperson contributes to the effectiveness of the message/information being disseminated. Objective and credible information should serve to: 1) control destructive rumors, 2) reduce anticipatory anxiety, and 3) return a sense of control to victims. Without breaching issues of confidentiality, the assembled group should receive factual information concerning that which is known and that which is not known regarding the crisis event.

PHASE THREE: The next step is to have credible healthcare professionals (if available) discuss the most common *reactions* (signs, symptoms, and psychological themes) that are relevant to the particular crisis event. For example, in the case of a suicide, the psychological theme of suicide should be addressed. In the case of terrorism, the dynamics of terrorism should be discussed. Common signs and symptoms of grief, anger, stress, survivor guilt, and even responsibility guilt among survivors, friends, and others should also be addressed.

PHASE FOUR: The final component of the CMB is to address personal coping and self-care strategies that may be of value in mitigating the distressing reactions to the crisis event. Simple and practical *stress management* strategies should be discussed. Community and organizational *resources* available to facilitate recovery should also be introduced. Questions should be actively entertained as appropriate.

Each group participant should leave the CMB with a reference sheet that briefly describes common signs and symptoms, common stress management techniques, and local professional resources (with contact names and telephone numbers) available to recovery.

Timing for the CMB is highly situation-specific and flexible. The CMB can be repeated as long as it proves to be useful.

Summary

This paper has introduced the "crisis management briefing" (CMB) as an efficient large group crisis intervention that may be used for primary civilian populations (and perhaps others) in the wake of terrorism, mass disasters, violence, and similar large-scale "community," school, organization, and community-wide crises. While the CMB, and similar interventions have been in use for years and have been anecdotally reported to be effective, the goal of this paper is to move toward a standardization of such procedures. With standardization comes reliability in application/implementation. In the final analysis, meaningful outcome research and its replication is based upon the reliable implementation of tactical protocols. Clearly, the overall effectiveness of the CMB should be submitted to controlled outcome investigations. This is a needed direction for the future. The human resource is the most valuable resource any organization or community possesses. The CMB is designed to protect that resource.

References

Ayalon, O. (1993). Posttraumatic stress recovery of terrorist survivors. In J. Wilson & B. Raphael (Eds). *International handbook of traumatic stress syndromes* (pp. 855-866). NY: Plenum.

Dyregrov, A. (1997). The process of psychological debriefing. *Journal of Traumatic Stress, 10*, 589-604.

Everly, Jr., G.S., & Piacentini, A. (1999, March). Effects of CISD on stress and trauma symptoms: A meta-analysis. *APA-NIOSH Work, Stress, and Health '99 Conference,* Baltimore.

Everly, Jr., G.S., Boyle, S., & Lating, J. (1999). The effectiveness of psychological debriefings in vicarious trauma: A meta-analysis. *Stress Medicine, 15*, 229-233.

Everly, Jr., G.S., & Boyle, S. (1999). Critical Incident Stress Debriefing (CISD): A Meta-Analysis. *International Journal of Emergency Mental Health, 1*(3), 165-168.

Everly, Jr.,G.S., & Mitchell, J.T. (1999). *Critical Incident Stress Management (CISM): A new era and standard of care in crisis intervention (2nd Ed.).* Ellicott City, MD: Chevron.

Everly, Jr.,G.S., Flannery, Jr., R.B., & Eyler, V. (2000, April). Effectiveness of a crisis intervention: A meta-analysis. Invited paper presented to the Third International Conference of Psychological and Social Services in a Changing Society, Kuwait City, State of Kuwait.

Everly, Jr.,G.S., Flannery, Jr., R.B., & Mitchell, J.T. (1999). Critical Incident Stress Management (CISM): A review of literature. *Aggression and Violent Behavior: A Review Journal, 5*, 23-40.

Flannery, Jr., R.B., Penk, W., & Corrigan N. (1999). Assaulted staff action program (ASAP): and declines in the prevalence of assaults: Community-based replication. *International Journal of Emergency Mental Health, 1*(1), 19- 22.

Flannery, Jr., R.B. (1998). *The Assaulted Staff Action Program: Coping with the psychological aftermath of violence.* Ellicott City, MD: Chevron Publishing.

Miller, L. (1999). Critical Incident Stress Debriefing: Clinical applications and new directions. *International Journal of Emergency Mental Health, 1*(4), 253-266.

Mitchell, J.T. & Everly, Jr., G.S. (in press). CISM and CISD: Evolution, effects, and outcomes. In B. Raphael & J. Wilson (Eds.), *Psychological Debriefing.*

Mitchell, J.T. & Everly, G.S. (1996). *Critical Incident Stress Debriefing: An operations manual for the prevention of raumatic stress among emergency sevices and disaster personnel* (2nd Ed.). Ellicott City, MD: Chevron.

Rose, S. & Bisson, J. (1998). Brief early psychological intervention following trauma: A systematic review of the literature. Journal of Traumatic Stress, *11*, 697-710.

Schreiber, J. (1978). *The Ultimate Weapon.* NY: Morrow.

Simon, J.D. (1994). *The Terrorist Trap.* Bloomington, IN: Indiana University Press.

<u>*Notes*</u>

Section Seven

DEFUSINGS

DEFUSING

Definition: A shortened version of the debriefing.

Length of Time: 20-45 minutes is the usual length. Debriefings usually take 2-3 hours.

Best Applied: Must be provided within 8 hours of an incident. If possible, it should be provided immediately (one to two hours) after the incident.

Target: Small groups of emergency workers, usually six to eight people. Multiple defusings for different groups of emergency workers (nurses, paramedics, police officers, fire fighters, etc.) may be provided for the same incident. Examples of usual target groups are engine companies, ambulance crews, emergency room staff, police squads, tactical units, and specialty teams.

Provided By: Trained Critical Incident Stress team members **only**.

Location of Defusing: Neutral environment free of distractions.

Goals:
1. Mitigate the impact of the event.
2. Accelerate the recovery process.
3. Assess of the need for debriefings and other services.
4. Reduce cognitive, emotional and physiological symptoms.

Process:
1. Establish a non-threatening social environment.
2. Allow rapid ventilation of the stressful experience.
3. Equalize the information cells.
4. Restore cognitive processing of the event.
5. Provide information for stress survival.
6. Affirm the value of the personnel.
7. Establish linkages for additional support.
8. Develop expectancies for the future.

Contraindications:
1. Usually not applied to disasters, except as part of a larger CISM program and only for small groups that have experienced extremely stressful circumstances.
2. Demobilizations are often utilized for large scale incidents and may be used instead of defusings.
3. Should only be used in a line of duty death when a formal debriefing team is not immediately available. Then great caution must be applied.

Defusings and demobilizations substitute for each other. One or the other is provided for the incident, not both.

Defusings outnumber the formal debriefings almost two to one.

A well run defusing will accomplish one of two things:
   a. A defusing may eliminate the need to provide a formal debriefing.
   b. A defusing will improve the willingness of the personnel to communicate in the formal debriefing if one is necessary.

The defusing is made up of three parts, unlike the debriefing which has seven segments.

People in a defusing may speak or be silent. There is no condition that would imply a requirement to speak.

No note taking or recording is allowed.

Occasionally, it is necessary to combine various groups of emergency personnel (police, fire, nursing, emergency medical) together for a defusing. This is only done when all the parties were involved together in the incident.

Defusing Components:
1. Introduction
2. Exploration
3. Information

Introduction:
- Introduce Facilitator
- State purpose
- Motivate participants
- Set rules
- Stress confidentiality
- Reassure participants it is not an investigative process
- Finish the process
- State goals
- Describe process
- Offer additional support

Exploration:
- Ask personnel to describe what just happened
- Ask a few clarifying questions
- Share experiences and reactions
- Assess need for more help
- Reassure as necessary

Information:
- Accept/summarize their exploration
- Normalize experiences and/or reactions
- Teach multiple stress survival skills
- Stress importance of diet & the need to avoid alcohol, fat, sugar & salt
- Rest/family life
- Recreation/exercise

Many teams have been making more frequent use of defusings with good results. ICISF strongly encourages the use of defusings. They are more immediate and less complicated than debriefings. They occur when the group members' emotional guards are down and their needs are high. Groups in crisis are more open to help (the right kind at the right place and time). Defusings carefully provided at the right time may lessen or eliminate the need to do a full debriefing. Teams that use defusings regularly report that the debriefings that follow are usually better (more powerful) than the debriefings provided without the benefit of the defusing. We would benefit from a formal study on that issue, but until one is completed, the clinical impressions are very positive in favor of defusings.

Defusings are small group meetings conducted within 8 hours of the conclusion of the event. They are conducted at a facility away from the scene – never at the scene. If a delay beyond 8 hours occurs, it is best not to do the defusing but to plan for a debriefing and, to provide individual services until the debriefing occurs. An exception to the 8 hour rule is in a line of duty death or some exceptionally distressing event. In that case, 12 hours may be a more useful cut off time. However, it is recommended that in line of duty deaths, a full fledged debriefing is provided instead of the defusing. In the case of a disaster, the demobilization (de-escalation) is a direct substitute for the defusing. One or the other is provided, not both.

A defusing is aimed at the core working group that was most seriously affected by the event i.e., a nursing unit, a truck company, a SWAT team, an ambulance crew. In most cases, it is best to provide a separate defusing for each of the groups involved in the event. On occasion, it may be necessary to provide one defusing for all of the agencies involved in the incident. A decision on a combined or separate defusing is up to the CISM team providing the defusing process.

Defusings may be provided by teams of peers, chaplains and mental health professionals, depending on the circumstances of the event. The defusing is an opportunity to observe the symptoms of distress and make some decisions as to whether or not a debriefing is going to be required.

If the personnel in the debriefing have "unfinished business," very intense reactions to the traumatic experience or no reaction whatsoever, these conditions may suggest that the need for a full 7 phase CISD.

Follow-up services are always necessary after a defusing to assure that the personnel are managing their stress adequately.

OBSERVING A DEFUSING

1.   The defusing has three (3) separate stages. As you observe the defusing, write a
        brief summary of what you saw happening within each of the defusing stages.

        Introduction -

        Exploration -

        Information -

2.   What was the role of the leader in each of the stages?

3.   What outcome was achieved at the end of the defusing?

Section Eight

CRITICAL INCIDENT STRESS DEBRIEFING

THE CRITICAL INCIDENT STRESS DEBRIEFING PROCESS (CISD) AND THE PREVENTION OF OCCUPATIONAL POST-TRAUMATIC STRESS

George S. Everly, Jr., Ph.D.

By many estimations, post-traumatic stress disorder (PTSD) represents the most severe and disabling variation of occupational stress known (Everly, 1989). Breslau, et al (1991) have noted that its prevalence may reach close to 9% of the young adult population in the U.S. Yet, at this time there exists no generally agreed upon "treatment of choice" for PTSD. The severity, prevalence, and lack of generally agreed upon therapeutic interventions all strongly argue for the development of a program to prevent PTSD in high risk populations. Critical Incident Stress Debriefing (Mitchell, 1983) is a form of psychological debriefing developed by one the authors (JTM) as a method for mitigating the harmful effects of work-related trauma and ultimately preventing PTSD.

Critical Incident Stress Debriefing (CISD) may be the most widely used group technique in the world for the prevention of work-related PTSD among high risk emergency response personnel. There exist nearly 700 quick response Critical Incident Stress Management teams across the globe.

This paper will describe the development of CISD, its basic elements, and its 10 year operational history as a preventive intervention for PTSD among high risk occupational groups.

BACKGROUND

Critical Incident Stress Debriefing (CISD) and its parallel process traumatic stress "defusing" are techniques initially developed by one of the authors (JTM) for the prevention of post-traumatic stress among high-risk occupational groups, specifically fire suppression, law enforcement, emergency medicine, disaster response, emergency dispatch and public safety personnel (Mitchell, 1983; 1988a, 1988b, 1991). These processes have subsequently been adopted by the military, the clergy, and pupil personnel services as well as within high risk business and industrial settings, (e.g., the banking industry, airlines, mining, oil discovery and refining operations, life guard services, and other recreational industries.) The employee assistance (EAP) industry has begun to heavily utilize the defusing and CISD and other processes, as well.

Adapted from a paper presented to the Second APA and NIOSH Conference on Occupational Stress. Nov. 19-22, 1992, Washington. D.C.

At the time of this writing, there exist over 700 formal trauma response teams across the globe which utilize the CISD and defusing models in the prevention of post-traumatic stress. CISD and defusing protocols have been employed for over 10 years in settings that range from small scale traumatic incidents to large scale disasters. CISD protocols have been employed in numerous major trauma venues.

The seeds of critical incident stress teams were actually planted during combat situations in World Wars I and II. Salmon (1919), Brown (1918) and Appel et al (1946) found that soldiers in the great wars were more prone to return to combat when given immediate psychological support after combat then when managed later in hospitals where they were well behind the combat lines.

More recently the Israeli Defense Forces began to utilize group and individual psychological support after fire fights in the Middle East. They concluded that the incidence of psychiatric disturbance was trimmed by as much as sixty percent since the inception of these support services (Breznitz, 1980).

The earliest CISM teams were begun in fire and emergency medical services units (Mitchell, 1983). There now exist over 700 CISD teams designed to mitigate the adverse impact of crisis and trauma upon high risk occupational groups.

THE CISM TEAM

Critical Incident Stress Teams are in actuality a partnership between mental health professionals and emergency or other high risk workers who are interested in preventing and mitigating the negative impact of acute stress on themselves and other workers. They are also interested in accelerating the recovery process once an emergency person or a group has been seriously stressed or traumatized.

Mental health professionals who serve on the teams have at least a masters degree in psychology, social work, psychiatric nursing, or mental health counseling. They are specially trained in crisis intervention, stress, post-traumatic stress disorder, and the critical incident stress debriefing process.

Peer support personnel are drawn from emergency service organizations, police, fire, emergency medical services, dispatch, disaster response personnel, and nurses (especially those in emergency or critical care centers) and other high risk occupational groups with specialized training. Both the mental health professionals and peer support personnel form a pool of critical incident team members from which a response team is developed. An incident which is predominantly police oriented is worked by police peers with the support of mental health professionals who are familiar with police activities and procedures.

Likewise an incident that is predominantly fire in nature will have fire peers who provide the support services, etc. If an incident involves various response agencies then a mixed cadre of peers is developed to provide support services.

CISD DEFINED

The CISD and defusing processes may be defined as group meetings or discussions about a traumatic event, or series of traumatic events. The CISD and defusing processes are solidly based in crisis intervention theory and educational intervention theory. The CISD and defusing processes are designed to mitigate the psychological impact of a traumatic event, prevent the subsequent development of a post-traumatic syndrome, and serve as an early identification mechanism for individuals who will require professional mental health follow-up subsequent to a traumatic event.

The formal CISD process is a seven stage intervention. These stages are delineated in Table 1 (Mitchell and Everly, 1996).

Table 1

STAGES OF CISD

Objectives

Stage 1	Introduction	To introduce intervention team members, explain process, set expectations.
Stage 2	Fact	To describe traumatic event from each participant's perspective on a cognitive level.
Stage 3	Thought	To allow participants to describe cognitive reactions and to transition to emotional reactions.
Stage 4	Reaction	To identify the most traumatic aspect of the event for the participants and identify emotional reactions.
Stage 5	Symptom	To identify personal symptoms of distress and transition back to cognitive level.
Stage 6	Teaching	To educate as to normal reactions and adaptive coping mechanisms, i.e., stress management. Provide cognitive anchor.
Stage 7	Re-Entry	To clarify ambiguities, prepare for termination, facilitate "psychological closure," i.e., reconstruction.

(see Mitchell and Everly, 1997 for step-by-step guidelines).

The debriefing process has both psychological and educational elements, but it should not be considered psychotherapy. Instead, it is a structured group meeting or discussion in which personnel are given the opportunity to discuss their thoughts and emotions about a distressing event in a controlled, structured, and rational manner. They also get the opportunity to see that they are not alone in their reactions but that many others are experiencing the same reactions.

As noted above, the debriefing is structured with seven major phases. It has been carefully structured to move in a nonthreatening manner from the usual cognitively oriented processing of human experience that is common to high risk professional personnel through a somewhat more emotionally oriented processing of these same experiences. The debriefing concludes by returning the personnel to the cognitive processing of their experiences.

POST-TRAUMA DEFUSING DEFINED

The defusing process is typically a three stage intervention. It may be considered a shortened version of the CISD. Defusings are designed to be:

a) implemented immediately, or within 8 hours of a traumatic event;
b) shorter in length than a formal CISD (about 1 hour compared to a 2-3 hour CISD);
c) more flexible than a CISD (greater latitude in the three-stage format); and,
d) used to either eliminate the need for a formal CISD, or enhance a subsequent CISD.

The stages of a defusing are delineated in Table 2 (Mitchell and Everly, 1997).

Table 2
Stages of Post-Trauma Defusings

		Objectives
Stage 1	Introduction	To introduce intervention team members, explain process, set expectation
State 2	Exploration	To discuss the traumatic experience via participants' disclosure of facts, cognitive and emotional reactions, and finally symptoms of distress related to the traumatic event
Stage 3	Information	To cognitively normalize and educate with regard to stress, stress management and trauma

(see Mitchell and Everly, 1997 for step-by-step guidelines).

Mechanism of Action

CISD and defusing interventions appear to derive their effectiveness from several aspects of their phenomenology:

1) EARLY INTERVENTION. CISD is most typically utilized as an early intervention strategy, often employed within hours of the traumatic event. Thus, the CISD is mobilized before traumatic memories may be concretized and perhaps distorted and over-generalized.

2) OPPORTUNITY FOR CATHARSIS. Catharsis refers to the ventilation of emotions. CISD provides a safe, supportive, structured environment wherein individuals can ventilate emotions. In a review of studies specifically investigating the relationship between the disclosure of traumatic events and stress arousal, Pennebaker and Susman (1988) concluded that disclosure of traumatic events leads to reduced stress arousal and improved immune functioning.

3) OPPORTUNITY TO VERBALIZE TRAUMA. CISD not only gives individuals the opportunity to release emotions, but the opportunity to verbally reconstruct and express specific traumas, fears and regrets. van der Hart, Brown and van der Kolk (1989) recount the views of master traumatologist Pierre Janet who noted at the turn of the 20th Century that the successful treatment of post-traumatic reactions was largely based upon the patient's ability to reconstruct and integrate the trauma using the verbally expressive medium, as well as express feelings (catharsis).

4) STRUCTURE. CISD provides a finite behavioral structure, i.e., a group debriefing represents a finite beginning and a finite end, superimposed upon a traumatic event representing chaos, suffering, and a myriad of unanswered questions.

5) GROUP SUPPORT. CISD, in its classic application, employs a group education model. The value of using a group format to address distressing issues is well documented. Yalom (1985) notes that the group format provides numerous healing factors intrinsic to the group format itself. Among them are the exchange of useful constructive information, catharsis, the dissolution of the myth of a unique weakness among individuals, the modeling of constructive coping behavior, the opportunity to derive a sense of group caring and support, the opportunity to help oneself by helping others and, perhaps most importantly with regard to trauma, the generation of feelings of hope.

6) PEER SUPPORT. Although mental health professionals oversee the CISD process, it is peer-driven. Carkhuff and Truax (1965) long ago demonstrated the value of lay support models. Indeed, peer support interventions offer unique advantages over traditional mental health services, especially when the peer-group views itself as being highly unique, selective, or otherwise "different" compared to the general population.

7) OPPORTUNITY FOR FOLLOW-UP. The CISD process represents an entry portal where potential victims can engage in group discussion, information exchange, and support. It also represents a mechanism wherein individuals who do require formal psychological care can be identified and helped so as to maximize the likelihood of rapid and total recovery.

SUMMARY

Critical Incident Stress Debriefing and its parallel intervention, post-traumatic stress defusing, are interventions designed by one of the authors (Mitchell, 1983; 1988a; 1988b; 1991) specifically for the prevention of post-traumatic stress and PTSD among high risk occupational groups such as fire fighters, emergency medical personnel, law enforcement personnel, public safety, dispatch personnel, and disaster workers. The modified CISD appears especially suited for mass disasters and community response applications.

The 10 year period since their origination has revealed significant proliferation and expanding applications worldwide. The efforts of Mitchell and Everly (1993; 1996) represent the only major source of operational "how to" guidelines for implementing CISD and defusing interventions. Although there is a paucity of controlled research, it is hoped that the future will see research efforts and applications expand.

CISD PROCESS

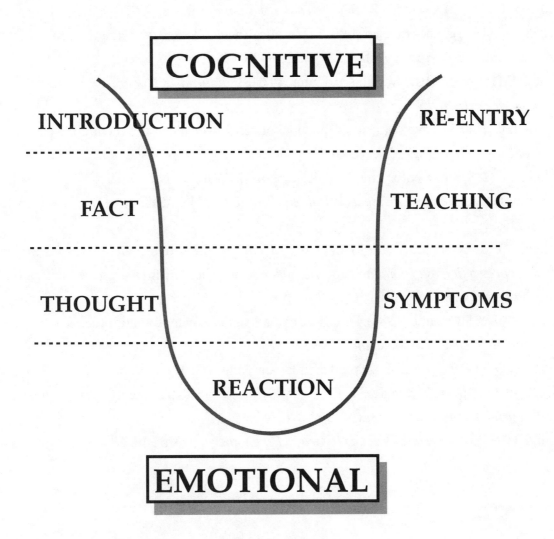

REFERENCES

Appel, J. W., Beebe, G. W. & Hilgardner, D.W. (1946). Comparative incidence of neuropsychiatric casualties in World War I and World War II. *American Journal of Psychiatry, 102,* 196-199.

Breslau, N., Davis, G.C. & Andreski, P. (1991). Traumatic events and post-traumatic stress disorder in an urban population of young adults. *Archives of General Psychiatry, 48,* 216-222.

Breznitz, S. (1980). Stress in Israel. In. H. Selye (Ed.) *Selye's Guide to Stress Research.* (pp. 71-89). New York: Van Nortrand Reinshold Co.

Brown, M. W. and Willliams (1918). *Neuropsychiatry and the war: A bibliography with abstracts.* New York: National Committee for Mental Hygiene.

Carkhuff, R. & Traux C. (1965). Lay mental health counseling. *Journal of Consulting Psychology, 29,* 426-431.

Everly, G. (1989). *A clinical guide to the treatment of the human stress response.* New York: Plenum Press.

Herman, J. L., (1992). Complex PTSD. *Journal of Traumatic Stress,* 5, 377-392.

Mitchell, J. T. (1983). When disaster stikes...The critical incident stress debriefing process. *Journal of Emergency Medical Services, 8,* 36-39.

Mitchell, J. T. (1988a). History, status and future of CISD. *Journal of Emergency Medical Services, 13,* 49-52.

Mitchell, J. T. (1988b). Development and functions of a critical incident stress debriefing team. *Journal of Emergency Medical Services, 13,* 43-46.

Mitchell, J. T. (1991). Law enforcement applications of critical incident stress debriefing teams. In J. T. Reese (Ed.), *Critical Incidents in Policing* (pp. 289-302). Washington, DC: U.S. Department of Justice.

Mitchell, J. T. & Everly, G. S. (1993). *Critical incident stress debriefing: An operations manual for the prevention of trauma among emergency service and disaster workers.* Baltimore, Maryland: Chevron Publishing.

Pennebaker, J. & Susman, J. (1988). Discosure of traumas and psychosomatic processes. *Social Science, and Medicine, 26,* 327-332.

Salmon, T. W. (1919). War neuroses and their lesson. *New York Medical Journal, 109,* 993- 994.

van der Hart, O., Brown, P. & van der Kolk, B. (1989). Pierre Janet's treatment of post-traumatic stress. *Journal of Traumatic Stress, 2,* 379-396.

Talom, I. (1985). *Theory and Practice of Group Psychotherapy* (3rd ed.). New York: Basic Books.

INTRODUCTORY REMARKS FOR
DEFUSINGS AND CISD

The following remarks may be used by a CISM team to introduce a Critical Incident Stress Debriefing or a defusing. It is not necessary to state each item in each defusing or debriefing. These general remarks cover the main introductory points for both defusings and CISD. It is best that the concepts presented in this outline be given to a group in the words of the team. They should not be read to the group from these pages. At times, it may be necessary to add additional comments not shown here. This can be done at the discretion of the team. The order of the presentation of the items is not of major importance. What is important is that the basic guidelines are presented by the CISM team during the introductory phase of the debriefing.

- Team leader identifies self.*

- We are here because of (describes or names the critical incident).*

- Some of you do not want to be here. You feel you don't need a debriefing. Please remember even if you don't need help, others present here may. Please stay. You may be able to help some of the people in this room simply by your presence. Please try to be helpful to one another.

- Some of you feel you can handle this on your own. That is probably true. However, experience demonstrates that people who try to handle everything alone take longer to do it.*

- A critical incident is any event that is extraordinary and produces significant reactions in emergency personnel. The critical incident is so unusual that it overwhelms the usual, normal abilities emergency personnel have developed to cope with a situation.

- The CISD (or defusing) process is designed to lessen the overall impact of an event and to accelerate recovery in normal people who are having normal reactions to abnormal events.*

- We have found that people who talk about a bad incident eat better, sleep better, remain healthier, stay on the job longer, and do not have as much disruption in their home lives.

- The CISD (or defusing) process is a discussion of an unusual event but it is not a critique or part of an investigation.*

- No notes are allowed. Neither do we allow recordings of what is said and the representatives of the media are never allowed.

- Everything that is said in this room is confidential. **(Heavily emphasize confidentiality).**

    Nothing leaves this room.*

* = core items

- You will be asked to speak two times in the CISD. The first time we ask each of you to tell us who you are, what your role was at the incident, and what happened during the incident. In the second question we will ask if you could cite your first thought once you stopped functioning on "automatic pilot."

- You do not have to speak at any time if you do not wish to. However, we do not recommend that because it can do more harm than good. We recommend instead that you talk about the incident.

- Our main job is to get you back in service and keep you as healthy and satisfied as possible. We are not here to take you out of service. We are here to listen to you and to help as best as we can.*

- You may ask any questions you wish and we'll try to help you out with some practical and useful information. Please ask any question anytime you wish.

- Please speak only for yourself. You cannot possibly speak adequately for how someone else is reacting.*

- Remember, confidentiality is the key. We need to have a pact of trust between all of us. Everyone has already been hurt enough. Don't use anything you learn or hear in this room except information the team teaches you about stress.*

- We do not want anyone to make judgment about anyone else. Every person has his own perspective. Let each state it without judgment.*

- We will not take any breaks. If you have to take care of your personal needs during the debriefing do so quietly and then return to this room. Leaving and not returning to this session may be harmful to you. Much of what we discuss at the end of the session is extremely valuable information that may be helpful. We don't want you to miss it so please hang in there with us.*

- Please look around the room and point out anyone who does not belong in this room. The CISM team members will briefly raise their hands so that you might more easily identify them. Anyone else who you don't recognize please point out and we will challenge that person's presence. If an officer was at the scene he or she belongs here. In the case of line of duty death, the entire department belongs in one of these sessions.

- No one has any rank during this session. We are all just people trying to struggle through some pain and make some meaning out of a chaotic situation so forget your rank and be a person first.

- We will be around at the end of the session. If you want to talk to us, feel free. We are here for you. Anything you can't tell us in the group you are welcome to tell us alone.*

- We will begin in just a moment by asking you to tell us about the incident.

- We would appreciate your turning off your pagers, cell phones and radios to help avoid distractions.

- One final reminder about *confidentiality* before we get into the facts of the situation. Let's keep whatever is heard here in this room confidential.*

- We'll have a handout or two at the end of the session.

- The next phase of the CISD, the fact phase, is now ready to begin.

Detailed procedures for the remainder of the CISD phases can be found in the *CISD Operations Manual, 3rd edition,* (Mitchell and Everly, 2001).

KEY CONCEPTS - CISD

- Crisis intervention is not psychotherapy

- CISD is group crisis intervention, not group psychotherapy.

- CISD is structured conversation or discussion of a traumatic event

- Goals: 1. Mitigate impact of a crisis/traumatic event
  2. Accelerate normal recovery processes in normal people who are experiencing normal reactions to totally abnormal events

- Peer support and mental health professionals are used in combination:
  - **Mental health professional always required**
  - Peer frequently used in emergency services, hospital based, military, airlines and disaster field workers debriefings
  - Peer not always required for commercial, business and industrial settings depending on circumstances

- _**ALL**_ CISM team members must be trained to provide the CISD process regardless of background and other types of training.

- Seven phase process

  1. INTRODUCTION
  2. FACT
  3. THOUGHT
  4. REACTION
  5. SYMPTOMS
  6. TEACHING
  7. RE-ENTRY

- One to two hours ideal for a debriefing but the process is dependent on size of the group and may last longer.

- All team members are active in process.

- Avoid probing and psychotherapeutic interpretation.

- Use homogenous groups.

- Facilitate group discussion.

- Explain the difference between privilege vs. confidential.

- Focus on participants' needs not the team's needs.

- Re-entry phase is the most important for gaining "closure."

- Do not argue with perceptions.

- Provide information and people can change their own perceptions.

- Deal only with material brought out by the participants.

- Avoid detailed operational or investigative information.

- CISD is not a critique of the incident.

- Stick with the model.

- Confidentiality is vital.

- Do not take notes.

- Provide follow-up.

- Reserve debriefing for serious events.

- Remember the group is normal, not pathological.

- Keep debriefing conversational and flowing.

- Do not theorize, moralize, psychologically interpret, or judge.

- Team should listen, stabilize, inform, normalize and recover.

- Do not engage in telling "war stories."

- Team members talk actively in the beginning and at the end, less in reaction phase.

- Teach according to the needs of the group and make teaching practical.

- Provide immediate follow up with the most seriously affected personnel.

- Understand the guidelines for referral.

- **Be familiar with and follow guidelines in CISD manual.**

OBSERVING A DEBRIEFING EXERCISE

1.   The CISD has 7 separate stages. Write down what happened during the CISD, which you observed, that indicated the beginning of each of the stages listed below:

    1. Introduction -

    2. Fact -

    3. Thought -

    4. Reaction -

    5. Symptom -

    6. Teaching -

    7. Re-entry -

2.   Who was in control of the CISD? What things were done which indicated control?

    Verbal -

    Non-verbal -

3. The CISD not only progresses through each of the 7 functional phases, it also progresses psychologically from the Cognitive (thought) Domain to the Affective (emotional) Domain and back to the Cognitive Domain. Indicate what happened to initiate the beginning of each of these domains:

Cognitive Domain -

Affective Domain -

Cognitive Domain -

4. Did the debriefing achieve a sense of psychological closure to the critical incident described? If so, how? If not, why not?

5. If you were the team leader for the debriefing you just observed, what would you plan to do at the end of the debriefing?

<u>*Notes*</u>

Section Nine

COMMON
MISTAKES

CRITICAL INCIDENT STRESS MANAGEMENT GROUP PROCESS

TYPE	DEMOBILIZATION	DEFUSING	DEBRIEFING CISD	CRISIS MANAGEMENT BRIEFING
WHEN	After Shift	Within 12 hours	24 hours - 10 days*	Anytime post-crisis
WHO	Large # of responders	Small groups	Small groups	Organizations/Schools Communities
FORMAT	Information & Rest	3 Stages	7 Stages	Information & Resources
LEADER	Peer, chaplain mental health	Peer, chaplain or mental health	At least one mental health trained leader	Peer, chaplain and/or mental health
LENGTH	½ hour	20 - 45 minutes	1½ -3 hours	1 - 1½ hours
FOLLOW-UP**	CISD	Assess need for CISD	Closure or referral	Assess need for CISD

*Debriefings for disasters may not be appropriate until 2-4 weeks (and sometimes longer) following the disaster.

** During and following all group processes the need for 1:1 follow-up is always assessed.

Joyce LiBethe, Ph.D.

SERIOUS CISD MISTAKES

If a debriefing is going to fail, it is likely to fail on one of the following items. Some of these mistakes can cause harm to the participants in a debriefing. All of these mistakes should be carefully avoided.

- Using untrained CISM team members

- Not using mental health professionals in a debriefing

- Misunderstanding the CISD process that progresses from strongly cognitive . (***Introduction*** and ***Fact*** phases) to a transition phase from cognition to affect (***Thought*** phase) to a strongly affective phase (***Reaction***) and finally back through a transition phase (***Symptoms***) to cognition phases again (***Teaching*** and ***Re-Entry***). See the table below:

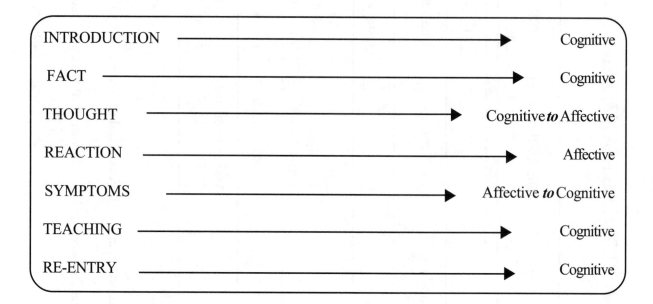

- Attempting to turn CISD into psychotherapy

- Attempting to substitute CISD for psychotherapy

- Not utilizing CISD trained peers for emergency, hospital, military or other operational groups

- Not preparing adequately for debriefing

- Not arriving early enough to circulate around and meet the participants

- Not doing an adequate case review

- Not having a CISD team strategy meeting before the debriefing

- Picking a team full of inexperienced debriefers

- Picking a team member with significant current personal problems

- Not providing appropriate follow-up services after the CISD

- Not meeting after a debriefing to make sure the CISM team is okay

- Not assessing the need for appropriate CISD (Underuse of the process)

- Overusing CISD by utilizing the process on minor events

- Not following the CISD model significantly

- Altering the CISD model

- Telling "war stories" during a debriefing

- Not looking periodically at other team members during a debriefing in order to communicate nonverbally.

- Writing notes during a debriefing

- Arguing with the participants

- Acting or speaking in a manner that indicates insensitivity to the participants

- Bringing up information from other debriefings

- Breaking confidentiality

Notes

Section Ten

NARRATIVE AND STATISTICAL REVIEWS

Continuing Education

CRISIS INTERVENTION: A REVIEW

Raymond B. Flannery, Jr., Ph.D. and George S. Everly, Jr., Ph.D.

ABSTRACT: *Critical incidents are sudden, unexpected, often life-threatening time-limited events that may overwhelm an individual's capacity to respond adaptively. Frequently, extreme critical incident stressors may result in personal crises, traumatic stress, and even Posttraumatic Stress Disorder. This paper presents a concise, fully-referenced, state-of-the-art review of crisis intervention procedures within the context of Critical Incident Stress Management (CISM; Everly & Mitchell, 1999; Flannery, 1999). [International Journal of Emergency Mental Health, 2000, 2(2), 119-125].*

KEYWORDS: Crisis; crisis intervention; Critical Incident Stress Management (CISM); disaster

The field of crisis intervention is predicated upon the existence of the phenomenon of psychological crisis. Because crisis intervention is the natural corollary of the psychological crisis, this review begins with a definition of the crisis phenomenon.

The Nature of a Crisis

A crisis occurs when a stressful life event overwhelms an individual's ability to cope effectively in the face of a perceived challenge or threat (Auerbach & Kilmann, 1997; Everly & Mitchell, 1999; Raphael, 1986; Sandoval, 1985; Schwartz, 1971; Wollman, 1993). More specifically, a crisis may be thought of as a response condition wherein: 1) psychological homeostasis has been disrupted; 2) one's usual coping mechanisms have failed to reestablish homeostasis; and, 3) the distress engendered by the crisis has yielded some evidence of functional impairment (Caplan,

Raymond B. Flannery, Jr., Ph.D., Massachusetts Department of Mental Health and Harvard Medical School; and, George S. Everly, Jr., Ph.D., Loyola College in Maryland and The Johns Hopkins University. Address correspondence concerning this article to: Raymond B. Flannery, Jr., Ph.D., Department of Psychiatry, The Cambridge Hospital, 1493 Cambridge Street, Cambridge, MA 02139

1961, 1964; Everly & Mitchell, 1999). If a crisis is a response, then what term defines the stressor event?

The term "critical incident" is a term which is frequently confused with the term crisis. Contrary to the crisis response, a critical incident may be thought of as any stressor event that has the potential to lead to a crisis response in many individuals. More specifically, the critical incident may be thought of as the stimulus that sets the stage for the crisis response.

Of particular importance to emergency mental health (EMH) are extreme stressor critical incidents such as disasters and human acts of violence that may result in psychological trauma and Posttraumatic Stress Disorder (PTSD; American Psychiatric Association, 1994; Everly & Lating, 1995; Flannery, 1994, 1995). Traumatic crises or critical incidents may occur in the face of actual or threatened death, serious injury, or some other threat to the victim's physical integrity. Individuals may also be victimized by witnessing these events occurring to others (American Psychiatric Association, 1994). Crises may also emerge as the result of a contradiction to some deeply held belief (Everly & Lating, 1995).

Frequently, victims of these traumatic events

experience disruptions in reasonable mastery of the environment, in caring attachments to others, and in sustaining a purposeful meaning in life (Butcher, 1980; Flannery, 1994; Raphael, 1986; Sandoval, 1985; Wollman, 1993). Victims may also experience the common symptoms of hypervigilance, sleep disturbance, intrusive recollections of the event, and a tendency to withdraw from full participation in daily activities (Butcher, 1980; Flannery, 1994, 1998; Mitchell & Everly, 1996). The impact of traumatic events may be profound and may last until death if these events are left untreated [See this journal, Continuing Education Series: *Psychological trauma and Posttraumatic Stress Disorder: A review* (1999, 1, 135-140) for a complete discussion of these matters].

Crisis Intervention:
A Definition

Over the years, crisis intervention has proven an effective, front-line intervention for victims of all types of critical incidents, especially the extreme stressors that may result in psychological trauma (Everly, Flannery, & Mitchell, 2000; Everly & Mitchell, 1999). Crisis intervention is defined as the provision of emergency psychological care to victims as to assist those victim's in returning to an adaptive level of functioning and to prevent or mitigate the potential negative impact of psychological trauma. (Everly & Mitchell, 1999).

Crisis intervention procedures have evolved from the studies of grieving conducted by Erich Lindemann (1944) in the aftermath of a major nightclub conflagration, from the military writings of Kardiner and Spiegel (1947) on the three basic principles in crisis work–immediacy of interventions, proximity to the occurrence of the event, and the expectancy that the victim will return to adequate functioning–and Gerald Caplan's emphasis (1964) on community mental health programs that emphasize primary and secondary prevention.

Therefore, in sum, intervention should be the natural corollary of the nature of the given problem. As such, the term "crisis intervention" should parallel the conceptualization of the term crisis. Consistent with the formulations of Caplan (1961, 1964), crisis intervention may be thought of as urgent and acute psychological intervention. The hallmarks of these first interventions are:
1) immediacy,
2) proximity,
3) expectancy, and,
4) brevity.
Furthermore, the goals of crisis intervention are:
1) stabilization, i.e., cessation of escalating distress;
2) mitigation of acute signs and symptoms of distress; and,
3) restoration of adaptive independent functioning, if possible; or, facilitation of access to a higher level of care.

Crisis Intervention:
Basic Principles

While there is no one single model of crisis intervention (Jacobson, Strickler, & Mosley, 1968), there is common agreement on the general principles to be employed by EMH practitioners to alleviate the acute distress of victims, to restore independent functioning and to prevent or mitigate the aftermath of psychological trauma and PTSD (Butcher, 1980; Everly & Mitchell, 1999; Flannery, 1998; Raphael, 1986; Robinson & Mitchell, 1995; Sandoval, 1985; Wollman, 1993).

1.   INTERVENE IMMEDIATELY. By definition, crises are emotionally hazardous situations that place victims at high risk for maladaptive coping or even for being immobilized. The presence on-site of EMH personnel as quickly as possible is paramount.

2. STABILIZE. One important immediate goal is the stabilization of the victims or the victim community actively mobilizing resources and support networks to restore some semblance of order and

routine. Such a mobilization provides the needed tools for victims to begin to function independently.

3. FACILITATE UNDERSTANDING. Another important step in restoring victims to pre-crisis level of functioning is to facilitate their understanding of what has occurred. This is accomplished by gathering the facts about what has occurred, listening to the victims recount events, encouraging the expression of difficult emotions, and helping them understand the impact of the critical event.

4. FOCUS ON PROBLEM-SOLVING. Actively assisting victims to use available resources to regain control is an important strategy for EMH personnel. Assisting the victim in solving problems within the context of what the victim feels is possible enhances independent functioning.

5. ENCOURAGE SELF-RELIANCE. Akin to active problem-solving is the emphasis on restoring self-reliance in victims as an additional means to restore independent functioning and to address the aftermath of traumatic events. Victims should be assisted in assessing the problems at hand, in developing practical strategies to address those problems, and in fielding those strategies to restore a more normal equilibrium.

Crisis Intervention: Agents of Change

Although the beneficial outcomes in crisis intervention may be due to traditional agents of change such as group cohesion, catharsis, imitative behavior, and the sharing of information (Yalom, 1985), authors who study crisis intervention procedures (Busutill et al., 1995; Everly & Mitchell, 1997; Flannery, 1998; Pennebaker, 1990, 1993, 1999; Raphael, 1986; Shalev, 1994; Tehrani & Westlake, 1994; Wollmann, 1993) have proposed with remarkable unanimity three factors considered important as agents of change in crisis procedures: ventilation and abreaction, social support, and adaptive coping.

An ability to share the negative emotional impact of a traumatic event is seen as an important step in recovery. Being able to share the horror of these critical incidents permits the victim to share the fear, understand the impact of the event, and begin the process of independent functioning. Similarly, social support networks provide victims with support, companionship, information, and instrumental assistance in beginning again. Adaptive coping is the third likely agent of change, and includes both cognitive and behavioral skills with an emphasis on information gathering, cognitive appraisal, reasonable expectations of performance, and skill acquisition.

These three agents of change may be attained in the five principles noted above, and should guide the efforts of EMH practitioners.

Crisis Intervention: Critical Incident Stress Management

A relatively new term that has emerged in the crisis intervention literature within the last decade is "Critical Incident Stress Management." (CISM; Everly & Mitchell, 1999; Flannery, 1999). CISM is a comprehensive crisis intervention system consisting of multiple crisis intervention components which functionally span the entire temporal spectrum of a crisis. CISM interventions range from the pre-crisis phase through the acute crisis phase, and into the post-crisis phase. CISM is also considered comprehensive in that it consists of interventions which may be applied to individuals, small functional groups, large groups, families, organizations, and even entire communities.

As currently evolved, CISM (Everly & Mitchell, 1999) includes numerous core elements: 1) pre-crisis preparation; 2) large scale demobilization procedures for public safety personnel as well as large group crisis management briefings for civilian victims of terrorism, mass disaster, community crises, school system tragedies and the like; 3) individual acute crisis intervention; 4) brief small group discussions, called defusings to assist in acute symptom reduction; 5) longer small group discussions known as Critical Incident Stress Debriefings (CISD; Mitchell & Everly, 1996); 6) family crisis intervention procedures; 7) organizational development interventions; and, 8) referrals for additional psychological assessment and treatment where indicated. CISM (Everly & Mitchell, 1999) allows the EMH practitioner to tailor the intervention response to individual or organizational needs and is emerging as the international standard of care for victims.

Variations of the CISM model have been adopted by numerous and diverse organizations in a wide variety of workplace settings including the Federal Aviation Administration (FAA), the United States Air Force, the United States Coast Guard, the US Secret Service, the Federal Bureau of Investigations (FBI), the Bureau of Alcohol, Tobacco, and Firearms (ATF), the Airline Pilots Association (ALPA), the Swedish National Police, the Association of Icelandic Rescue Teams, the Australian Navy, and the Massachusetts Department of Mental Health.

Crisis Intervention: Research Findings

Single Interventions

The evaluation of CISM actually began, historically, with a narrowly focused evaluation of psychological debriefings, choosing to extract the debriefing process from the overall multifaceted CISM formulation.

While some studies (e.g., Bisson, Jenkins, Alexander, & Bannister, 1997; Kenardy, Webster, Levin, Carr, Hazzell, & Cater, 1996; McFarlane, 1988) have found either partial or no support for debriefing interventions, many of these studies have had serious methodological research issues. In some studies, the type of debriefing interventions is not clear, the training of the EMH providers is not described, and the tools used to evaluate the

effectiveness of the debriefing interventions are inadequate. In some cases, the effectiveness of the debriefing was measured several months after the debriefing was provided, a period of time in which the victims could have been exposed to additional traumatic events. As an addendum, it should be noted that a recent and oft-cited paper, referred to as the Cochrane Review (Wessley, Rose, & Bisson, 1998), has called for the cessation of "mandatory debriefing" as a crisis intervention. It is important to note that 1) the Review actually failed to asses the group debriefing process known as CISD, the evidence cited was based upon "individual" debriefings clearly not the industry standard, and 2) the Review failed to assess CISM or any other multicomponent CISM-like system.

Given these methodological shortcomings, it would be inaccurate to generalize from singular CISD investigations so as to reach any conclusion regarding CISM. Nevertheless, as recent meta-analytic reviews have demonstrated (Everly, Boyle, & Lating, 1999; Everly and Boyle, 1999; Everly and Piacentini, 1999) when the intervention model is clear, when the EMH personnel are correctly trained, and the assessment procedure for effectiveness is adequate, then even a limited array of crisis intervention procedures are found to be effective in helping victims (Bohl, 1991; Bordow & Porritt, 1979; Brom, Kleber, & Hofman, 1993; Bunn & Clark, 1979; Chemtob, Tomas, Law & Cremmiter, 1997; Flannery, 1998; Hokanson, 1997; Jenkins, 1996; Leeman-Conley, 1996; Nurmi, 1999; Raphael, 1977; Wee, Mills, & Koehler, 1999; Western Management Consultants, 1996). Well controlled studies continue to be sought.

Multiple Intervention Programs: CISM

To date, there is no common agreement on which of the CISM components (Everly & Mitchell, 1999) should be the minimum standard in any multicomponent approach, but the following examples demonstrate the versatility of this

CISD- stress debriefing

approach.

Everly and Mitchell (1999; Mitchell, Schiller, Eyler, & Everly, 1999) have used the core CISM components in developing a comprehensive approach for the victims of natural and man-made disasters as well as for the EMH staff that render services in these times of community crisis. These multiple components not only provide support to victims and emergency services personnel, but also serve as a screening procedure for individuals who need further assistance (Everly & Mitchell, 1999).

Flannery and his colleagues (Flannery, 1998, 1999) have developed a CISM approach (Everly & Mitchell, 1999) for healthcare providers of child and adult services in emergency rooms, inpatient, outpatient, day programs, homeless shelters, and community-based residents. The model includes individual crisis counseling, CISD (Mitchell & Everly, 1996) group debriefings, staff victim support groups, staff victim family counseling, and professional referral, when indicated. This approach has provided needed support to employee victims and has resulted in sharp declines in facility-wide violence as well as dollar cost savings in terms of less sick leave, less medical and legal expense, less industrial accident claims, less staff turnover, and sustained productivity.

Leeman-Conley (1996) developed a multicomponent approach for bank personnel subject to armed robberies. Her approach includes pre-incident preparedness, training managers to support employee victims, individual crisis intervention, group debriefings, and long-term counseling. Sick leave was reduced by sixty percent, and workers compensation claims were lowered by sixty-eight percent.

Tehrani and her coworkers (Tehrani, 1995) addressed the needs of postal employee victims. Her model includes manager debriefings, individual crisis counseling of employee victims, and long-term trauma counseling, if indicated. Her approach has provided needed support to employee victims in times of crisis.

Busuttil and his colleagues (Busuttil et al., 1995) employed a multicomponent CISM-like crisis intervention in the wake of conflict-related trauma and found it effective in reducing PTSD-like symptoms.

Finally, Richards (1999) found the CISM system of crisis intervention superior in the reduction of PTSD-like symptoms in civilian bank employees when compared to CISD alone subsequent to the critical incident of bank robberies.

With specific regard to the multifaceted CISM, empirical reviews both narrative (Everly, Flannery, & Mitchell, 1999) and especially meta-analytic (Everly, Flannery, and Eyler, 2000) suggest CISM to be an effective crisis intervention capable of reducing the acute manifestations of distress associated with crisis. Randomized experimental designs are still unfortunately lacking and are needed. The use of meta-analytic scrutiny of CISM does serve to diminish the limitations of the current quasi-experimental investigations by reducing the likelihood of systematic experimental bias across studies, however. Nevertheless, randomized investigations are still sought.

Each of these programs illustrate the power of CISM approaches (Everly & Mitchell, 1999) to address the emergency mental health service needs of a variety of work site settings. The flexibility of the model permits each crisis response team to employ a variety of interventions based on the current and changing needs of the organization and the crisis event.

Crisis Intervention: Implications

The evidence for the occurrence of critical incidents worldwide is compelling. These emergencies are frequent, and no nation or group of people is exempt from these events. Equally clear from these studies is the intense human suffering, physical injury and death, and accompanying psychological trauma and PTSD in the surviving victims of, or witnesses to, these critical incidents.

This suffering suggests the need for preventive and treatment interventions in the hands of skilled EMH specialists. This review has documented the mounting empirical evidence that the multicomponent crisis intervention strategies of the CISM approach (Everly & Mitchell, 1999) do in fact provide the tools for both prevention and corrective treatment.

The need for CISM as well as other EMH teams and for research on the nature and outcomes of these interventions is widespread. Senior managers are needed for the fielding and evaluation of crisis intervention systems. The potential for disasters and human acts of violence is an ongoing problem as is the cultural denial of the potential for these critical incidents. This attitude is not correct and may consign individuals to unnecessary suffering as victims. Senior managers are in an important position to bolster EMH teams and needed research, and to address the cultural denial. EMH personnel should actively elicit the support of senior managers so that the extent and quality of EMH services that they provide to victims is enhanced.

References

American Psychiatric Association (1994). *The diagnostic and statistical manual of mental disorders* (4th Ed.). Washington, DC: American Psychiatric Press.

Auerbach, S. & Kilmann, P. (1997). Crisis intervention: A review of outcome research. *Psychological Bulletin, 84,* 1189-1217.

Bisson, J., Jenkins, P., Alexander, J., & Bannister, C. (1997). Randomized controlled trial of psychological debriefing for victims of acute burn trauma. *British Journal of Psychiatry, 171,* 78-81.

Bohl, N. (1991). The effectiveness of brief psychological interventions in police officers after critical incidents. In Reese, J., Horn, J., & Dunning, C. (Eds.). *Critical incidents in policing.* Washington, DC: US Government Printing Office, 31-88.

Bordow, S. & Porritt, D. (1979). An experimental evaluation of crisis intervention. *Social Science and Medicine, 13,* 251-256.

Brom, D., Kleber, R., & Hofman, M. (1993). Victims of traffic accidents: Incidence and prevention of Post-Traumatic Stress Disorder. *Journal of Clinical Psychology, 49,* 131-140.

Bunn, T.A. & Clarke, A.M. (1979). Crisis intervention: An experimental study of the effect of a brief period of counseling on the anxiety of relatives of seriously injured or ill hospital patients. *British Journal of Psychology, 52,* 191-195.

Busuttil, A., Turnbull, G., Neal, L., Rollins, J., West, A., Blanch, N., & Herepath, R. (1995). Incorporating psychological debriefing techniques within a brief therapy programmer for the treatment of Posttraumatic Stress Disorder. *British Journal of Psychiatry, 167,* 495-502.

Butcher, J.N. (1980). The role of crisis intervention in an airport disaster plan. *Aviation, Space, and Environmental Medicine, 51,* 1260-1262.

Caplan, G. (1961). *An approach to community mental health.* New York: Grunne & Stratton.

Caplan, G. (1964). *Principles of preventive psychiatry.* New York: Basic Books.

Chemtob, C., Tomas, S., Law, W., & Cremmiter, D. (1997). Post-disaster psychosocial intervention: A field study of the impact of debriefing on psychological distress. *American Journal of Psychiatry, 154,* 415-417.

Everly, Jr., G.S. & Boyle, S. (1999). Critical Incident Stress Debriefing (CISD): A meta-analytic review of effectiveness. *International Journal of Emergency Mental Health, 1*(3), 165-168.

Everly, Jr., G.S. & Lating, J.T, Eds. (1995). *Psychotraumatology: Key papers and core concepts in post-traumatic stress.* New York: Plenum.

Everly, Jr., G.S. & Mitchell, J.T. (1999). *Critical Incident Stress Management (CISM): A new era and standard of care in crisis intervention* (2nd Ed.). Ellicott City, MD: Chevron Publishing.

Everly, Jr., G.S., & Quatrano-Piacentini, A. (1999, March). The effects of CISD on trauma symptoms: A meta-analysis. Paper presented to the APA-NIOSH Conference on Work, Stress, and Health in a Global Economy, Baltimore, MD.

Everly, Jr., G.S., Boyle, S., & Lating, J. (1999). The effectiveness of psychological debriefings in vicarious trauma: A meta-analysis. *Stress Medicine, 15,* 229-233.

Everly, Jr., G.S., Flannery, Jr., R.B., & Eyler, V. (2000, April). Effectiveness of a comprehensive crisis intervention system: A meta-analysis. Invited paper presented to the Third International Conference, Psychological & Social Services in a Changing Society. Kuwait City, State of Kuwait.

Everly, Jr., G.S., Flannery, Jr., R.B., & Mitchell, J.T. (2000). Critical Incident Stress Management: A review of literature. *Aggression and violent behavior: A review journal, 5,* 23-40.

Flannery, Jr., R.B. (1994). *Post-Traumatic Stress Disorder: The victim's guide to healing and recovery.* New York: Crossroad Press.

Flannery, Jr., R.B. (1995). *Violence in the workplace.* New York: Crossroad Press.

Flannery, Jr., R.B. (1998). *The Assaulted Staff Action Program: Coping with the psychological aftermath of violence.* Ellicott City, MD: Chevron Publishing.

Flannery, Jr., R.B. (1999). Critical Incident Stress Management and the Assaulted Staff Action Program. *International Journal of Emergency Mental Health, 1*(2), 103-108.

Hokanson, M. (1997, April). Evaluation of the effectiveness of Critical Incident Stress Management Program for the Los Angeles County Fire Department. Paper presented at the Fourth World Congress on Stress, Trauma, and Coping in the Emergency Services Professions, Baltimore.

Jacobson, G., Strickler, M., & Morley, W. (1968). Generi and individual approaches to crisis intervention. *American Journal of Public Health, 58,* 338-343.

Jenkins, S.R. (1996). Social support and debriefing efficacy among emergency medical workers after a mass shooting incident. *Journal of Social Behavioral and Personality, 11,* 477-492.

Kenardy, J.A., Webster, R.A., Levin, T.J., Carr, B.J., Hazell, P., & Cater, G.L. (1996). Stress debriefing and patterns of recovery following a natural disaster. *Journal of Traumatic Stress, 9,* 37-49.

Kardiner, A. & Spiegel, H. (1947). *War, stress, and neurotic illness.* New York: Hoeber.

Leeman-Conley, M. (1990). After a violent robbery. . . *Criminology Australia*, April/May, 4-6.

Lindemann, E. (1944). Symptomology and management of acute grief. *American Journal of Psychiatry, 101,* 141-148.

McFarlane, A.C. (1988). The longitudinal course of posttraumatic morbidity: The range of outcomes and their predictors. *The Journal of Nervous and Mental Disease, 176,* 30-39.

Mitchell, J.T. & Everly, Jr., G.S (1996). *Critical Incident Stress Debriefing (CISD): An operations manual for the prevention of traumatic stress among emergency services and disaster workers.* Ellicott City, MD: Chevron Publishing.

Mitchell, J.T., Schiller, G., Eyler, V.A., & Everly, Jr., G.S. (1999). Community crisis intervention: The Coldenham tragedy revisited. *International Journal of Emergency Mental Health, 1(4),* 227-236.

Nurmi, L. (1999). The sinking of the Estonia: The effects of Critical Incident Stress Debriefing on rescuers. *International Journal of Emergency Mental Health, 1(1),* 23-32.

Pennebaker, J.W. (1990). *Opening up.* New York: Avon.

Pennebaker, J.W. (1993). Putting stress into words: Health, linguistic, and therapeutic implications. *Behaviour Research and Therapy, 31* (6), 539-548.

Pennebaker, J.W. (1999). The effects of traumatic disclosure on physical and mental health. The value of writing and talking about upsetting events. *International Journal of Emergency Mental Health, 1*(1), 9-18.

Raphael, B. (1977). Preventive intervention with the recently bereaved. *Archives of General Psychiatry, 34,* 1450-1454.

Raphael, B. (1986). *When disaster strikes.* New York: Basic Books.

Richards, D. (1999, April). *A field study of CISD vs. CISM.* Paper presented to the Fifth World Congress on Stress, Trauma, and Coping in the Emergency Services Professions, Baltimore.

Robinson, R.C. & Mitchell, J.T. (1995). Getting some balance back into the debriefing debate. *The Bulletin of the Australian Psychological Society, 17,* 5-10.

Sandoval, J. (1985). Crisis counseling: Conceptualizations and general principles. *School Psychology Review, 14,* 257-265.

Schwartz, S. (1971). A review of crisis intervention programs. *Psychiatric Quarterly, 45,* 498-508.

Shalev, A.Y. (1994). Debriefing following traumatic exposure. In Ursano, R.J., McCoughey, B.G., & Fullerton, C.S. (Eds.). *Individual and community response to trauma and disaster: The structure of human chaos.* Cambridge: Cambridge University Press, 201-219.

Tehrani, N. & Westlake, R. (1994). Debriefing individuals affected by violence. *Counseling Psychology Quarterly, 7,* 251-259.

Tehrani, N. (1995). An integrated response to trauma in three post office businesses. *Work and Stress, 9,* 380-393.

Wee, D.F., Mills, D.M., & Koehler, G. (1999). The effects of Critical Incident Stress Debriefing on emergency medical services personnel following the Los Angeles civil disturbance. *International Journal of Emergency Mental Health, 1*(1), 33-38.

Wessley, S., Rose, S., & Bisson, J. (1998). A systematic review of brief psychological interventions (debriefing) for the treatment of immediate trauma related symptoms and the prevention of Posttraumatic Stress Disorder (Cochrane Review). *Cochrane Library, Issue 3.* Oxford.

Western Management Consultants (1996). *The Medical Services Branch CISM evaluation report.* Vancouver, BC: Author.

Wollman, D. (1993). Critical Incident Stress Debriefing and crisis groups: A review of the literature. *Group, 17,* 70-83.

Yalom, I. (1985). *The theory and practice of group psychotherapy.* (3rd Ed). New York: Basic Books.

CRITICAL INCIDENT STRESS DEBRIEFING (CISD): A META-ANALYSIS

George S. Everly, Jr., Ph.D. & Stephen H. Boyle

ABSTRACT: *Psychological debriefings represent a genre of group crisis interventions. Critical Incident Stress Debriefing (CISD) represents the oldest standardized variation of this genre. Recent reviews have called into question the effectiveness of CISD. In this study 5 previously published investigations were meta-analyzed revealing a large effect size (Cohen's d = .86) supporting the notion that the CISD model of psychological debriefing is an effective crisis intervention. [International Journal of Emergency Mental Health, 1999, 3, 165-168.]*

KEY WORDS: debriefing; CISD; crisis intervention' Critical Incident Stress Debriefing; Cohen'sd

Critical Incident Stress Debriefing (CISD) represents a group crisis intervention technique, originally developed by Mitchell (1983), designed to mitigate the acute symptoms of distress associated with psychological crisis and trauma. It is a guided and structured group discussion of a crisis or traumatic event. CISD employs the active mechanisms of early intervention, verbal expression, cathartic ventilation, group support, health education, and assessment for follow-up. CISD is the oldest variation, or "model," within the extant genre of psychological debriefing techniques.

CISD was designed to be only one component of a comprehensive multicomponent crisis intervention program referred to as Critical Incident Stress Management (CISM) (Everly & Mitchell, 1999). Since its initial development, CISD technology has enjoyed remarkable popularity because of its perceived efficiency and effectiveness. Although CISD was never designed to be implemented as a "one shot" intervention outside of the multicomponent CISM program (Everly & Mitchell, 1999; Mitchell & Everly, in press), crisis workers have, indeed, found it necessary upon occasion to implement CISD either outside of the context of a CISM framework, or with little contextual support. The purpose of this investigation was to assess the overall effectiveness of the CISD crisis intervention technology when it was implemented outside of the full multicomponent CISM.

There has been only one previously conducted meta-analysis of psychological debriefing as a group crisis intervention technique (Everly, Boyle, & Lating, in press). While the results supported the effectiveness of debriefing, the meta-analysis combined several different debriefing models.

Similarly, there have been various narrative reviews of the genre of psychological debriefing (Bisson & Deahl, 1994; Watts, 1994; Robinson & Mitchell, 1995; Raphael, Meldrum, & McFarlane, 1995; Raphael, Wilson, Meldrum, & McFarlane, 1997; Rose & Bisson, 1998; Dyregrov, 1998). The conclusions have been mixed with regard to the question of overall effectiveness. Unfortunately, the practical utility of some of these reviews and the validity of their conclusions have been compromised because of their failure to clearly define and distinguish the operational nature of the independent variable under scrutiny, i.e., the specific form, or model, of psychological debriefing used. A clear and restrictive definition of the independent variable is an essential feature of any review process (Mullen, 1989). Indeed, science itself is built upon clear and sharply defined concepts, variables, and taxonomies. In several of the aforementioned reviews, all debriefings were

---

George S. Everly, Jr., Ph.D., Loyola College in Maryland and The Johns Hopkins University. Stephen H. Boyle. University of Maryland Baltimore County. Address correspondence concerning this article to: George S. Everly, Jr., Ph.D., 702 Severnside Ave., Severna Park, MD 21146

aggregated on the basis of terminology alone without any apparent regard for differences in formal implementation protocols which serve to distinguish various debriefing models, variations in prescribed recipient constituencies, or any other operational factors which might serve to functionally differentiate between the numerous models of psychological debriefing.

In an attempt to clarify the conflicting conclusions surrounding the effectiveness of psychological debriefings, Everly and Mitchell focused solely upon the CISD model of psychological debriefing and offered narrative reviews of the effectiveness of specifically CISD (Everly & Mitchell, 1999; Mitchell & Everly, 1997). As Mullen (1989) cogently points out, however, even well-focused narrative reviews are subject to divergent interpretation. He offers, therefore, empirical meta-analysis as a more precise, objective, and compelling exercise in the conduct of inquiry. In the present study, meta-analysis was used in an effort to objectively assess the effectiveness of CISD.

Method

The combinatorial statistical procedure of meta-analysis was used in the present investigation to evaluate the overall effectiveness of CISD. Meta-analysis allows for the statistical integration of the results of independent investigations so as to summarize and statistically express the overall effectiveness of the intervention under investigation.

Relevant medical and psychological data bases dating back to 1990 were accessed using the key word indicators Critical Incident Stress Management, Critical Incident Stress Debriefing, CISD, debriefing, crisis intervention, and psychological debriefing in order to identify appropriate investigations for subsequent aggregation. Relevant conference proceedings were also included in the literature search.

Following the recommendations of Mullen (1989), a precise and highly restrictive definition of the independent variable was used in data extraction for subsequent inclusion in the meta-analysis. Only studies purporting to specifically assess the Critical Incident Stress Debriefing (CISD) model of group crisis intervention (Mitchell, 1983) were used, consistent with the narrative review and recommendations of Everly and Mitchell (1999). CISD appears to be the oldest of the psychological debriefing techniques and possesses an operational "manual" so as to ostensibly enhance the reliability of the CISD protocol across independent applications (Mitchell & Everly, 1995).

Subjects

Using the aforementioned selection criteria, five empirical investigations purporting to assess the effectiveness of CISD were identified and used. The five investigations yielded an aggregate subject pool of 341 adults.

Procedure

Initially, outcome measures were combined within each study submitted for meta-analysis. This yielded an average outcome statistic, or effect size, for each individual study. The effect size may be thought of as a statistical expression of how effective the CISD intervention proved to be within each individual investigation. In this meta-analysis, Cohen's d (Cohen, 1977) was chosen as the indicator of effect size. Cohen's d is the most commonly used index of statistical power for meta-analysis.

The effect sizes across studies were then combined using the weighted meta-analytic statistical approach developed by Mullen (1989). A singular weighted average effect size was then generated.

Next, the diffuse comparison of effects sizes (DCES) was calculated. The DCES serves as an estimation of the probability that the effect sizes combined within the meta-analysis were significantly heterogeneous and thus may be thought of as arising from different populations of study outcomes. Sources of heterogeneity may include significantly different sample groups, functionally different dependent variables, and/or significantly different interventions.

Finally, a fail-safe number was calculated. The fail-safe number is an estimate of the number of potentially overlooked investigations with an average effect size of zero that would need to be identified in order to bring the results of the current investigation to the "just significant" convention of $p=.05$.

Results

Pooling all study outcomes using the CISD model of group crisis intervention yielded a significant effect size, Cohen's d =.86. According to Cohen (1977) this represents a large effect size indicative of a beneficial outcome associated with the use of the CISD (Mitchell, 1983). The probability that such a finding might be derived by chance approaches zero (p<.0000000001). Table 1 on the next page summarizes the participant investigations of CISD effectiveness.

The DCES was not significant (p=.409) indicating that the effect sizes used in this investigation represent a homogeneous data set, despite the diversity of subjects, settings, and crisis events and thus warranted aggregation for the purposes of this meta-analytic investigation. The fail-safe number was estimated at 91.

Discussion

The purpose of the present investigation was to assess the effectiveness of the CISD group crisis intervention technology, originally developed by Mitchell (1983). The CISD intervention is one component of the comprehensive CISM crisis intervention system. The CISM system consists of seven integrated components designed to provide comprehensive crisis response capabilities covering the entire crisis spectrum from pre-crisis planning through acute crisis and post crisis interventions (Everly & Mitchell, 1997).

Although never designed to be a stand alone intervention, CISD has, indeed, been applied outside of the comprehensive CISM context. An analysis of its active mechanisms would certainly lead one to predict its ability to mitigate acute psychological distress, but narrative reviews are subject to varying interpretations, while the previous meta-analysis failed to isolate the CISD "model" of psychological debriefing. Thus, a more precise and objective meta-analysis was called for to address the issue of effectiveness as it relates to the application of CISD outside of the CISM context.

The results of the aggregated participant studies assessing the CISD intervention are compelling, indeed. A large effect size was revealed attesting to the power of the CISD to mitigate symptoms of psychological distress. This beneficial effect was revealed despite the wide variety of subject groups, the wide range of traumatic events, and the diversity of outcome measures.

Although only five studies purporting to assess CISD were discovered as a result of the literature search, the aggregated studies did contribute a substantial number of subjects (341) to the meta-analysis.

Clearly, a larger subject pool would have been desirable. Nevertheless, the results of this meta-analysis are encouraging. Having established the viability of CISD as a crisis intervention technology, further research needs to be directed toward the comprehensive CISM program of which CISD is only one component.

Finally, it is important to understand that the results of the current meta-analysis do not generalize nor do they serve to support other variations, or models, of psychological debriefing. These results are CISD-specific.

Table 1: Summary of CISD Effectiveness Studies

Study	CISD	Subjects	Measures	Cohen's d
Nurmi (1999)	Within 3-7 days of ferry sinking	133 emergency workers 105e; 28c	Impact of Events: Penn Inventory	.89
Jenkins (1996)	24 hours after mass shooting	29 emergency workers 15e; 14c	SCL-90 anxiety, depression repeated measures 8-10 days & 1 month post CISD	.93
Bohl (1991)	24 hours post critical incident	71 police personnel 40e; 31c	Beck Depression; STAL Novaco anger; stress sx 3 months post CISD	.86
Chemtob, et al, (1997)	6 & 9 months post-hurricane	43 adult victims Time-lagged design	Impact of events 90 days post CISD	1.37
Wee (1999)	1-14 days post LA riots	65 emergency medical technicians 42e; 23c	Frederick Reaction Index 3 months post CISD	.47

References

Bisson, J.I. & Deahl, M. (1994). Psychological debriefing and the prevention posttraumatic stress: More research is needed. *British Journal of Psychiatry, 165,* 717-720.

Bohl, N. (1995). The effectiveness of brief psychological interventions in police officers after critical incidents. In J. Reese, J. Horn, & C. Dunning (Eds.). Critical Incidents in Policing, Revised (pp. 31-38). Washington, DC: Department of Justice.

Chemtob, C., Tomas, S., Law, W., & Cremniter, D. (1997). Postdisaster psychosocial intervention: A field study of debriefing on psychological distress. *American Journal of Psychiatry, 134,* 415 - 417.

Cohen, J. (1977). Statistical power analysis for the behavioral sciences. NY: Academic Press.

Dyregrove, A. (1998). Psychological debriefing - an effective method? *Traumatology/e, 4* (2), Article one.

Everly, G.S. & Mitchell, J.T. (1999). Critical Incident Stress Management (CISM): A new era and standard of care in crisis intervention (2nd Edition). Ellicott City, MD: Chevron Publishing Corporation.

Everly, G.S., Boyle, S., & Lating, J. (in press). The effectiveness of psychological debriefing with vicarious trauma: A meta-analysis. *Stress Medicine.*

Jenkins, S.R. (1996). Social support and debriefing efficacy among medical workers after a mass shooting incident. *Journal of Social Behavior and Personality, 11,* 477-492.

Mitchell, J.T. (1983). When disaster strikes. . . The Critical Incident Stress Debriefing process. *Journal of Emergency Medical Services, 8,* 36-39.

Mitchell, J.T. & Everly, G.S. (in press). The CISD and CISM: Evolution, effects, and outcomes. In B. Raphael and J. Wilson (Eds.). Psychological Debriefing.

Mitchell, J.T. & Everly, G.S. (1995). Critical Incident Stress Debriefing (CISD): An operations manual for the prevention of traumatic stress among emergency services and disaster personnel. 2nd Ed, Revised. Ellicott City, MD: Chevron Publishing Corporation.

Mitchell, J.T. & Everly, G.S. (1997). Scientific evidence for CISM. *Journal of Emergency Medical Services, 22,* 87-93.

Mullen, B. (1989). Advanced BASIC MetaAnalysis. Hillsdale, NJ: Erlbaum.

Nurmi, L.A. (199). The sinking of the Estonia: The effects of Critical Incident Stress Debriefing (CISD) on rescuers. *International Journal of Emergency Mental Health, 1,* 23-31.

Raphael, B., Wilson, J., Meldrum, L., & McFarlane (1996). Acute preventive interventions. In B. vander Kolk, et al. (Eds.). Traumatic Stress (pp. 463-479). NY: Guilford.

Raphael, B., Meldrum, L., & McFarlane, A. (1995). Does debriefing after psychological trauma work? *British Medical Journal, 310,* 1479-1480.

Robinson, R. & Mitchell, J. (1995). Getting some balance back into the debriefing debate. *Bulletin of the Australian Psychological Society, 17,* 5-10.

Rose, S. & Bisson, J. (1998). Brief early psychological intervention following trauma: A systematic review of the literature. *Journal of Traumatic Stress, 11,* 697-710.

Watts, R. (1994). The efficacy of critical incident stress debriefing for personnel. *Bulletin of the Australian Psychological Society, 16,* 6-7.

Wee, D., Mills, D.M., & Koehler, G. (1999). The effects of Critical Incident Stress Debriefing (CISD) on emergency medical services personnel following the Los Angeles civil disturbance. *International Journal of Emergency Mental Health, 1,* 33-37.

Research

THE ASSAULTED STAFF ACTION PROGRAM (ASAP) AND DECLINES IN ASSAULTS: A META-ANALYSIS

Raymand B. Flannery, Jr., Ph.D., George S. Everly, Jr., Ph.D., and Victoria Eyler, M.S.

ABSTRACT: *Crisis intervention procedures have been demonstrated to be of assistance in addressing the aftermath of psychological trauma. The Assaulted Staff Action Program (ASAP) is a Critical Incident Stress Management (CISM) approach that has been associated with providing needed support to employee victims of patient assaults and sharp reductions in the frequency of assaults in facilities where ASAP has been properly fielded. The purpose of this study was to conduct a meta-analysis of the effectiveness of ASAP in reducing frequency of assault. Results yielded a highly statistically significant Cohen's d of 3.1 and fail safe number of 202. The implications for risk management are discussed [International Journal of Emergency Mental Health, 2000, 2(3), 143-149].*

KEY WORDS: Assaulted Staff Action Program; ASAP; Crisis Intervention; Critical Incident Stress Management; CISM; Meta-Analysis

Psychological trauma is an individual's physical and psychological response to a sudden, usually unexpected, potentially life threatening event over which the individual has no control, an event which would intensely frighten the average person (Flannery, 1994). Natural disasters, combat, physical and sexual abuse, and the like are common examples of events that may prove traumatic and result in symptoms of hypervigilance, exaggerated startle response, sleep disturbance, and general dysphoria (Everly & Lating, 1995). Without proper treatment, these symptoms may persist until death.

Practitioners of Emergency Mental Health (EMH) are commonly called upon to address the aftermath of these traumatic events. EMH personnel who are present during the acute phase of a crisis may encounter victims who are stunned or exhibit the aforementioned symptomatology. These victims often need an array of intervention services.

These intervention procedures have been demonstrated to be effective in addressing the distress associated with traumatic events and in mitigating or precluding the long-term effect known as Posttraumatic Stress Disorder (PTSD; Everly, Flannery, & Mitchell, 2000). The field of crisis intervention is moving beyond single interventions toward Critical Incident Stress Management programs (CISM; Everly & Mitchell, 1999). CISM programs represent an integrated, comprehensive multicomponent crisis intervention approach that span the complete crisis continuum from precrisis and acute crisis phases to the postcrisis phase that may be of assistance to EMH personnel.

The Assaulted Staff Action Program (ASAP; Flannery, 1998) is a voluntary, system-wide, peer-help crisis intervention program designed to address the psychological sequelae experienced by many staff victims of patient assault. These assaults may

Raymond B. Flannery, Jr., Ph.D., Massachusetts Department of Mental Health. Address correspondence concerning this article to: Raymond B. Flannery, Jr., Ph.D. Department of Mental Health, 25 Stanford Street, Boston, MA 02114

occur as a result of staff conflicts about patient care (Stanton & Schwartz, 1954) as well as denial of services and acute intoxication (Flannery, 1998). ASAP is a prototypic CISM approach (Everly & Mitchell, 1999) in that it provides individual crisis interventions, group crisis interventions, a staff victims' support group, staff victim family crisis interventions, and individual referrals, as indicated. ASAP has been associated with providing needed support to staff victims (Flannery, 1998) and sharp declines in the frequency of assaults in six of seven facilities where ASAP has been fielded properly (Flannery, Hanson, Penk, Flannery, & Gallagher, 1995; Flannery, Hanson, Penk, Goldfinger, Pastva, & Navon, 1998; Flannery, Penk, & Corrigan, 1999; Flannery, Anderson, Marks, & Uzoma, 2000). The declines in assaults suggest the possible importance of ASAP as a basic risk management strategy.

The original decline in frequency of assaults after fielding the ASAP program was first observed in a 400-bed state mental hospital with 415 direct care nursing personnel on 13 patient care sites (Flannery, Hanson, Penk, Flannery, & Gallagher, 1995). These sites included three admissions units, three treatment units, and four transition-to-community units. There were 397 patients who were primarily Caucasian (90%), between the ages of 30-40 years, and were diagnosed with schizophrenia (85%), affective disorder (10%) or other (5%). Most were unemployed (90%) and involuntarily committed (90%). These characteristics did not change during the course of this study. The staff had access to medical, behavioral, and forensic consultation throughout this study. All staff were trained in nonviolent self-restraint procedures, alternatives to restraint and seclusion, and effective communication with patients.

The dependent variable in this study was any incident of patient assault. Patient assaults were of four types and included physical and sexual assaults, nonverbal intimidation, and verbal threats. This study employed a single case experimental design (Hersen & Barlow, 1976) in a pre- and post-test design in which the hospital served as its own control before

and after the fielding of ASAP. Prior to ASAP, the hospital had a baserate of 30 assaults per month. Twenty-two months later when this facility was closed due to downsizing, the rate of assault was 11 per month. This decline in frequency of assaults was statistically significant by student's t (t = 16.47; df = 8; p < .005).

The second study replicated the original finding in each of three additional state mental hospitals (Flannery, Hanson, Penk, Goldfinger, Pastva, & Navon, 1998). Hospital A was a 175-bed facility with 261 direct care staff on 5 patient care sites. Hospital B was a 175-bed unit with 295 direct care staff on 10 patient care sites. Hospital C was a 190-bed unit with 384 direct care staff on 8 patient care sites. The characteristics of the patient population and the resources and training of the staff were similar to those in the original study and were consistent throughout the duration of the study.

The dependent variable was again any incident of the four types of assaults noted above. This study utilized a multiple baseline design in which each facility served as its own control in a pre- and post-test design (Hersen & Barlow, 1976). These hospitals came online at staggered three-month intervals as an ASAP team was fielded at each site. Baserate data was gathered for three months prior to coming online. Assault data were gathered in each facility at quarterly intervals for the first twelve months post-ASAP. Prior to ASAP, the three hospitals combined had a baserate of 31 assaults per month. The assault frequency declined to 3.56 during the first quarter after ASAP was fielded and to 2.44 at the end of the fourth quarter. A repeated measures ANOVA revealed a statistically significant decline between the quarters before and after ASAP (F = 80. 85; df = 4, 40; p < .001). Post hoc Dunnett's tests revealed no significant differences between the first and other quarters.

The third study assessed the possible impact of an ASAP program in a 16-bed acute care unit of a community mental health center with 32 direct care staff (Flannery, Penk, & Corrigan, 1999). Training and services available to staff were similar to the two earlier studies. The characteristics of the patients in this study were individuals who were primarily Caucasian (90%), whose average age was approximately 35 years, and who had diagnoses of schizophrenia (29%), affective disorder (39%), or other (32%). These characteristics and staff resources did not change during the course of the study.

The dependent variable was any incident of patient assault. This study used the single case experimental pre- and post-test design. The baserate prior to fielding ASAP was 11.25 incidents per quarter, which declined to 0 at the end of the sixth quarter. A student's t-test revealed an additional statistically significant decline in frequency of assault (t = 12.93; df = 30; p < .001). The t-test in this study was based upon the number of staff pre- and post ASAP and was less robust due to a single incident of assault post ASAP.

The final study included two additional independent efforts to replicate original findings (Flannery, Anderson, Marks, & Uzoma, 2000). One facility was a 16-bed acute care unit of a rural community mental health center with 38 direct care staff. The second was a 125-bed urban intermediate/extended care facility with 150 direct care staff on 5 patient care sites. The patients in both facilities were primarily Caucasian (90%) between the ages of 36-55 years, with diagnoses of schizophrenia (35%), affective disorder (32%), personality disorder (18%), or other (15%). The training of and resources available to staff were similar to those in the previous studies. There were no significant changes in patient characteristics or staff resources throughout the course of the study.

The dependent variable in each study was any incident of the four types of patient assaults. A single case pre- and post-test experimental design was utilized in each facility. The community mental health facility began with a baserate of 32 incidents per year which increased to 34 per year 12 months after ASAP was fielded. A student's test revealed no statistically significant decline (t = -0.07; df = 22; p < 0.47). The intermediate/extended care facility had a baserate of 33 assaults per year, which declined to 25 assaults for the 12 months after ASAP was fielded. A student's t revealed this to be a statistically significant decline (t = 1.94; df = 22; p < 0.035).

Although the findings noted above were statistically significant in six facilities, the individual significance in each facility that contributed to the positive outcome may have been due to factors less related to the fielding of an ASAP program. For example, the staff in a facility may have been highly motivated to field ASAP and the declines in assaults are due to both ASAP and high staff motivation.

Before ASAP can be accepted as a risk management strategy, the effects of possible idiosyncratic variables producing positive outcomes need to be considered and the overall power of the ASAP intervention assessed. One approach to achieve this goal is by means of meta-analysis (Mullen, 1989) in which the findings of all of the independent studies are examined to express the overall effectiveness of the ASAP intervention itself. Therefore, the purpose of the present study was to assess the effectiveness of the ASAP intervention in reducing frequency of assaults by means of the more objective, integrated meta-analysis of the independent ASAP outcome studies.

Method

Epistemological reviews by Cooper (1979) and Mullen (1989) argue that the aggregation of research investigations by way of the narrative review may be vulnerable to reviewer bias as well as a lack of appreciation for the relative size of any given effect that may be revealed. To compensate for these potential weaknesses in narrative reviews, these authors recommend the meta-analytic statistical review and this is the methodology incorporated in the present investigation.

Relevant medical and psychological data bases dating back to 1995 were accessed using the key word indicators Assaulted Staff Action Program,

ASAP, Critical Incident Stress Management, CISM, and crisis intervention in order to identify appropriate investigations for subsequent aggregation. Conference proceedings were not included in the literature search.

Following the recommendations of Mullen (1989), precise and highly restrictive definitions of both independent and dependent variables were used in data aggregation for subsequent inclusion in the meta-analysis. Firstly, only studies purporting to specifically assess interventions utilizing the ASAP formulation (independent variable), as described by Flannery (1998), were used. The fact that ASAP possesses an operational "manual" (Flannery, 1998), so as to enhance the reliability of the ASAP protocol across independent applications, was seen as a distinct clinical advantage. Secondly, objective behavioral outcome were considered preferable to subjective self-report dependent variables which are commonly evident in the psychological literature. The present investigation utilized patient assaults upon staff as the dependent variable across participant studies.

Subject Pool

Using the aforementioned selection criteria, five empirical investigations (subjects) purporting to assess the effectiveness of ASAP were identified and utilized.

Procedure

The effect size of these studies may be thought of as a statistical expression of how effective the ASAP intervention proved to be within each individual investigation. In this meta-analysis, Cohen's d (Cohen, 1977) was chosen as the indicator of effect size. Cohen's d is the most commonly used index of statistical power in the determination of effect size for meta-analysis. The results of each study were transduced to yield the Cohen's d statistical expression of effect size. The effect sizes across studies were then combined using the unweighted meta-analytic statistical approach developed by Mullen (1989). A singular average effect size was then generated.

Finally, a fail-safe number was calculated. The fail-safe number is an estimate of the number of potentially overlooked investigations with an average effect size of zero that would need to be identified in order to bring the results of the current investigation to the "just significant" convention of $p = .05$.

Results

Pooling all study outcomes utilizing the ASAP model of crisis intervention yielded a significant effect size, Cohen's d = 3.175. According to Cohen (1977), this represents a large effect size indicative of a beneficial outcome associated with the use of ASAP as the CISM system. The probability that such a finding might be derived by chance was found to be low ($p < .0001$).

The fail-safe number was found to be 202.95 and was then submitted to Rosenthal's (1979) recommended sufficiency criterion. This statistical formulation addresses the question "Are additional studies needed to establish the existence of the purported effect?" The sufficiency criterion was determined to be a fail-safe number of 45. The obtained fail-safe number was 202.95, and far exceeding the required sufficiency criterion, an outcome providing further empirical evidence as to the effectiveness of the ASAP as a CISM crisis intervention system.

Table 1 summarizes the participant investigations of ASAP effectiveness.

Discussion

The purpose of the present study was to test the effectiveness of ASAP in reducing frequency of assault in facilities where ASAP has been properly fielded (Flannery, 1998) by means of a meta-analysis. Five empirical investigations into the effectiveness of the ASAP as a CISM intervention approach (Everly & Mitchell, 1999) were statistically aggregated and meta-analyzed to serve as the methodology for the extant review. The participant studies were independent in that they used varied staff personnel, varied patient populations, and varied settings.

The results of the aggregated meta-analyzed studies assessing the ASAP intervention suggest ASAP may be a powerful intervention in reducing frequency of assaultive behavior. This beneficial effect was obtained across a wide range of subject groups in a wide variety of patient care units in both inpatient and community settings. While the number of studies examined is limited to date, the fail-safe number additionally suggests the strength of the findings.

It may be argued by some that a limitation to the present meta-analysis is the predominance of single case experimental designs in the constituent study pool. However, single case experimental designs offer potential insight into causal relationships. Their power is enhanced through the deliberate combination of independent investigations performed on large groups of subjects, across multiple and diverse settings, as well as through a sustained sensitivity to the respective threats to internal validity that may be engendered within each study. The aforementioned aggregation serves to reduce the risk of systematic experimental error and argues for the verity of the current findings.

ASAP has been associated with providing cost-effective, clinically efficacious support to employee victims (Flannery, 1998). ASAP is flexible in design and can be readily used by EMH personnel in a variety of settings other than those of health care. Police/corrections, schools/colleges, and corporate and industrial settings are some of the venues where ASAP interventions could be introduced. ASAP interventions may also be successfully fielded to address other types of potentially traumatizing events in addition to assaults. For example, ASAP interventions can be employed to provide support to victims of rapes, robberies, and natural or man-made disasters.

Moreover, the present meta-analytic findings suggest the importance of additionally considering ASAP as a risk management strategy for enhanced safety in health care and other worksites. As has been noted, ASAP is manualized (Flannery, 1998) and is readily fielded with a minimum allocation of resources. It appears to act as a deterrent to subsequent violence and results in greater safety in these settings for both patients and staff.

Table 1: Summary of ASAP Effectiveness Studies

Study	ASAP	Subjects	Measures	Statistics	Cohen's d
Flannery, et al., (2000)	Assaulted Staff Action Program (ASAP), within 20 minutes after patient physical assaults on staff	150 direct care staff assaulted at an intermediate/extended care facility: pre/post design	Assault Rate 1 year pre-intervention, 1 year post-intervention	$t = 1.94$ $p < 0.035$	.827 $p = .03$
Flannery, et al., (2000)	Assaulted Staff Action Program (ASAP), within 20 minutes after patient physical assaults on staff	38 direct care staff at a community mental health center: pre/post design	Assault Rate 1 year pre-intervention, 1 year post-intervention	$t = 0.07$ $p < .05$	-.029 $p = .53$
Flannery, et al., (1999)	ASAP, after patient physical assaults on staff (unspecified timing post-assault)	32 direct care staff from a community mental health center: pre/post-design	Assault Rate: repeated measures - 3 months pre-intervention, quarterly for next 18 months	$t = 12.93$ $p < .001$	4.72 $p < .0001$
Flannery, et al., (1998)	ASAP, after patient physical assaults on staff (unspecified timing post-assault)	940 direct care staff assaulted at three state mental hospitals: pre/post design	Assault Rate: repeated measures - 3 months pre-intervention, quarterly for following year	$R = .9433$ $p < .001$	5.68 $p < .0001$
Flannery, et al., (1995)	ASAP, within 20 minutes after patient physical assaults on staff	415 direct care staff at a state mental hospital: pre/post design	Assault Rate: 3 months pre-intervention, quarterly for 22 months post-intervention	$t = 16.47$ $p < .005$	11.65 $p < .0001$
					Mean Cohen's d=3.175, $p < .0001$

References

Cohen, J. (1977). *Statistical power analysis for the behavioral sciences*. New York: Academic.

Cooper, H.M. (1979). Statistically combining independent studies: A meta-analysis of sex differences in conformity research. *Journal of Personality and Social Psychology, 37,* 131-146.

Everly, Jr., G.S. & Lating, J.T. (Eds.) (1995). *Psychotraumatology: Key papers and core concepts in posttraumatic stress.* New York: Plenum

Everly, Jr., G.S., & Mitchell, J.T. (1999). *Critical Incident Stress Management (CISM): A new era and standard of care in crisis intervention.* Second Edition. Ellicott City, MD: Chevron Publishing.

Everly, Jr., G.S., Flannery, Jr., R.B., & Mitchell, J.T. (2000). Critical Incident Stress Management (CISM): A review of the literature. *Aggression and Violent Behavior, 5,* 23-40.

Flannery, Jr., R.B. (1999). *Posttraumatic Stress Disorder: The victim's guide to healing and recovery.* New York: Crossroad.

Flannery, Jr., R.B. (1998). The *Assaulted Staff Action Program (ASAP): Coping with the psychological aftermath of violence.* Ellicott City, MD: Chevron.

Flannery, Jr., R.B., Anderson, E., Marks L. & Uzoma, L. (2000). The Assaulted Staff Action Program (ASAP) and declines in rates of assault: Mixed replicated findings. *Psychiatric Quarterly, 71,* 165-175.

Flannery, Jr., R.B., Penk, W., & Corrigan, M. (1999). The Assaulted Staff Action Program (ASAP) and declines in the prevalence of assaults: Community-based replication. *International Journal of Emergency Mental Health, 1,* 19-22.

Flannery, Jr., R.B., Hanson, M.A., Penk, W., Goldfinger, S., Pastva, G., & Navon, M. (1998). Replicated declines in assault rates after the implementation of the Assaulted Staff Action Program. *Psychiatric Services, 49,* 241-243.

Flannery, Jr., R.B., Hanson, M.A., Penk, W., Flannery, G.J., & Gallagher, C. (1995). The Assaulted Staff Action Program: An approach to coping with the aftermath of violence in the workplace. In L. Murphy, R. Hurrell, S. Sauter, & G. Keita (Eds), *Job stress intervention* (pp. 189-212). Washington, D.C.: American Psychological Association.

Hersen, M., & Barlow, D. (1976). *Single-case experimental designs: Strategies for studying behavioral change.* New York: Pergammon.

Mullen, B. (1989). *Advanced BASIC meta-analysis.* Hillsdale, J: Erlbaum.

Rosenthal, R. (1978). The "file drawer" problem of tolerance for null results. *Psychological Bulletin, 86,* 638-641.

Stanton, A. & Schwartz, M (1954). *The mental hospital.* N.Y.: Basic Books.

EFFECTIVENESS OF A COMPREHENSIVE CRISIS INTERVENTION SYSTEM: A META-ANALYSIS

George S. Everly, Jr., Ph.D., F.A.P.M.
The Johns Hopkins University
and Loyola College in Maryland

Raymond B. Flannery, Jr., Ph.D.
Harvard Medical School

Victoria Eyler, M.S.
Loyola College in Maryland

ABSTRACT: *Crisis intervention has emerged over the last 50 years as a proven method for the provision of urgent psychological support in the wake of a critical incident or traumatic event. The history of crisis intervention is replete with singular, time-limited interventions. As crisis intervention has evolved, however, more sophisticated multicomponent crisis intervention systems have emerged. As they have appeared in the extant empirically-based literature, their results have proven promising, indeed. The purpose of this investigation was to empirically assess the overall effectiveness of integrated multicomponent crisis intervention using the combinatorial statistical procedure of meta-analysis.*

Invited paper presented to the Third International Conference, Psychological & Social Services in a Changing Society, Kuwait City, State of Kuwait, April 2000. Correspondence: George S. Everly, Jr., Ph.D. 702 Severnside Ave., Severna Park, MD 21146, USA.

Crisis intervention is a holistic approach based on the public health model of a "population at risk." This assumes that proper intervention at an opportune moment can prevent more serious problems from developing...Crisis intervention is a proven approach to helping people in the pain of an emotional crisis (APA, 1989, p. 2520). The purpose of this investigation was to examine the effectiveness of the latest innovation and generation of crisis intervention systems; the multicomponential Critical Incident Stress Management (CISM) system as described by authors such as Everly and Mitchell (1999) and Flannery (1999a, 1999b). In doing so, the quantitative combinatorial statistical method of meta-analysis

was employed as a means of assessing the overall magnitude of effectiveness of this crisis intervention.

The concept of CISM is historically grounded in crisis interventions such as Critical Incident Stress Debriefing (CISD) and the Assaulted Staff Action Program (ASAP).

CISD represents a group crisis intervention technique, originally developed by Mitchell (1983), designed to mitigate the acute symptoms of distress associated with psychological crisis and trauma. It is a guided and structured group discussion of a crisis or traumatic event. CISD employs the active mechanisms of early intervention, verbal expression, cathartic ventilation, group support, health education, and assessment for follow-up. CISD is the oldest variation or "model," within the extant genre of psychological debriefing techniques. A point that is often overlooked, however, is that the intervention program referred to as Critical Incident Stress Management (CISM, Everly & Mitchell, 1999). Since its initial development, the CISD technology has enjoyed remarkable popularity because of its perceived efficiency and effectiveness. Although the CISD was never designed to be implemented as a "one shot" intervention outside of the multicomponent CISM program (Everly & Mitchell, 1999) crisis workers have, indeed, found it necessary upon occasion to implement the CISD either outside of a complete CISM framework, or with little contextual support. The complete CISM crisis intervention system employs a multicomponential program consisting of small group crisis interventions (CISD, defusings), large group crisis interventions (demobilizations, crisis management briefings, "town meetings"), individual crisis counseling (face-to-face, telephonic), family crisis intervention, and mechanisms for follow-up and referral for formal assessment and/or psychotherapy (see Everly and Mitchell, 1999 for a complete review).

A prototypic CISM formulation is the ASAP system developed by Flannery and his colleagues (see Flannery, 11998). Initially developed for use by hospital personnel, the multicomponent ASAP program has been applied to community mental health clinics and educational settings. The ASAP intervention has been submitted to rigorous empirical scrutiny.

In recent years, there have been narrative reviews of various crisis intervention approaches (Bisson & Deahl, 1994; Everly & Mitchell, 1999; Watts, 1994; Mitchell & Everly, 1997; Robinson & Mitchell, 111995; Raphael, Meldrum, & McFarlane, 1995; Raphael, Wilson, Meldrum, & McFarlane, 11997). The conclusions have been mixed with regard the question of overall effectiveness. Unfortunately, the practical utility of these reviews and the validity of their conclusions, in the aggregate, have been compromised because of the heterogeneity of the actual interventions reviewed and the occasional failure to even clearly define and distinguish the operational nature of the independent variables under scrutiny, i.e., the specific form, or model, of psychological intervention utilized. A clear and restrictive definition of the independent variable is an **essential** feature of any review process (Mullen, 1989). Indeed, science itself is built upon clear and sharply defined concepts, variables and taxonomies.

In an attempt to offer greater clarity Everly, Flannery and Mitchell (1999) conducted and exhaustive narrative review of these issues. As Mullen (1989) cogently points out, however, even well-focused narrative reviews are subject to divergent interpretations. He offers, therefore, empirical meta-analysis as a more precise objective, and compelling exercise in the conduct of inquiry.

In an effort to address concerns regarding divergent qualitative interpretation, Everly and his colleagues performed a series of restrictive meta-analyses as to determine the effectiveness of the CISD small group crisis intervention. The results of these analyses clearly demonstrated the effectiveness of the CISD crisis intervention when implemented in a standardized manner by trained interventions (Everly, Boyle & Lating, 1999; Everly & Boyle, 1999; Everly & Piacentini, 1999).

Despite the demonstrated effectiveness of the CISD intervention, it will be recalled that CISD is but one element of an overall CISM program and that CISM is a comprehensive, integrated multicomponent crisis intervention system. The CISM intervention system spans the entire temporal spectrum of a crisis from pre-incident preparation, through the acute crisis and post crisis phases. The next logical step, therefore, was to assess the overall effectiveness of the comprehensive, integrated multicomponent CISM program.

METHOD

The combinatorial statistical procedure of meta-analysis was used in the present investigation to evaluate the overall effectiveness of CISM. Meta-analysis allows for the statistical integration of the results of independent investigations so as to summarize and statistically express the overall effectiveness of the intervention under investigation. This statistical expression is known as "effect size."

Relevant medical and psychological data bases dating back to 1990 were accessed using the key word indicators Critical Incident Stress Management, CISM, and crisis intervention in order to identify appropriate investigations for subsequent aggregation. Relevant conference proceedings were also included in the literature search.

Following the recommendations of Mullen (1989), a precise and highly restrictive definition of the independent variable was used in data extraction for subsequent inclusion in the meta-analysis. Only studies purporting to specifically assess interventions consistent with the Critical Incident Stress Management formulation were utilized, consonant with the narrative review and recommendations of Everly and Mitchell (1999; Mitchell & Everly, 1997). The fact that CISM possesses an operational "manual" so as to enhance the reliability of the CISM protocol across independent applications (Everly & Mitchell, 11999) was seen as a distinct clinical advantage.

Subject Pool

Using the aforementioned selection criteria, seven empirical investigations (subjects) purporting to assess the effectiveness of CISM were identified and utilized.

Procedure

The effect size may be thought of as a statistical expression of how effective the CISM intervention proved to be within each individual investigation. In this meta-analysis, Cohen's d (Cohen, 1977) was chosen as the indicator of effect size. Cohen's d is the most commonly used index of statistical power in thee determination of effect size for meta-analysis. The results of each study were transduced to yield the Cohen's d statistical expression of effect size.

The effect sizes across studies were then combined using the weighted meta-analytic statistical approach developed by Mullen (1989).

A singular weighted average effect size was then generated.

Finally, a fail-safe number was calculated. The fail-safe number is an estimate of the number of potentially overlooked investigations with an average effect size of zero that would need to be identified in order to bring the results of the current investigation to the "just significant" convention of $p=.05$.

RESULTS

Pooling all study outcomes utilizing the CISM model of crisis intervention yielded a significant effect size, Cohen's $d=3.71$. According too Cohen (1977) this represents a large effect size indicative of a beneficial outcome associated with the utilization of the CISM system. The probability that such a finding might be derived by chance approaches zero $(p,.00000000001)$.

The fail-safe number was found to be 868.

The fail-safe number was submitted to Rosenthaal's (1979) sufficiency criterion. This statistical formulation addresses the question "Are additional studies needed to establish the existence of purported effect?" The sufficiency criterion was determined to be a fail-safe number of 45. The obtained fail-safe number was 868, thus far exceeding the required sufficiency criterion and thereby providing sufficient empirical evidence as to the effectiveness of the CISM crisis intervention system.

Table 1 summarizes the participant investigations of CISM effectiveness.

DISCUSSION

The purpose of the present investigation was to assess the effectiveness of the CISM crisis intervention technology, as described by Everly and Mitchell (1999) and Flannery (1999a, 1999b). The CISM system consists of standardized and integrated components designed to provide comprehensive crisis response capabilities covering the entire crisis spectrum from pre-crisis planning through acute crisis and post crisis interventions (Everly & Mitchell, 1999).

The statistical text of meta-analysis was called for to address the issue of effectiveness as it relates to the effectiveness of the CISM system.

The results of the aggregated meta-analyzed participant studies assessing the CISM intervention are compelling, indeed. An extremely large effect size was revealed attesting to the power of the CISM to mitigate symptoms of psychological distress. This beneficial effect was revealed despite the wide variety of subject groups, the wide range of traumatic events, and the diversity of outcome measures.

Although only seven studies purporting to assess CISM were discovered as a result of the literature search, the fail-safe number of 868 argues compellingly that these studies represent sufficient magnitude as to attest to the effectiveness of CISM.

Finally, it is important to understand that the results of the current meta-analysis do not generalize nor do they serve to support other variations, or models, of crisis intervention. They are CISM-specific.

Table 1: Summary of CISM Effectiveness Studies

Study	CISM	Subjects	Measures	Primary Statistics	Weighted Cohen's d
Busuttil (1995)	Timing post trauma varied; War-related trauma and non-war related (i.e., post-disaster body handling, terrorist attack, traffic accidents, hostage situations and witnessing fatal accidents)	34 adults; repeated measure design 20 Active Military, 5 Ex-Military, 3 Military Dependents, 6 Civilians	Clinician Administered PTSD Scale-1 (CAPS-1) Total Intensity: repeated measures - pre-treatment, 6 weeks and endpoint (1 year)	X^2=27.034 p<.0001	3.94 p<.0001
Flannery (2000)	Assaulted Staff Action Program (ASAP)*, within 20 minutes after patient physical assaults on staff	150 direct care staff assaulted at an intermediate/extended care facility: pre-post design	Assault Rate 1 year pre-intervention, 1 year post-intervention	t = 1.94 p < 0.035	.827 p = .03
Flannery (1999)	ASAP, after patient physical assaults on staff (unspecified timing post-assault)	32 direct care staff from a community mental health center: pre/post-design	Assault Rate: repeated measures - 3 months pre-intervention, quaterly for next 18 months	t = 12.93 p < .001	4.72 p < .0001
Flannery (1998)	ASAP, after patient physical assaults on staff (unspecified timing post-assault)	940 direct care staff assaulted at three state mental hospitals: pre-post design	Assault Rate: repeated measures - 3 months pre-intervention, quarterly for following year	R = .9433 p < .05	5.68 p < .0001
Flannery (1995)	ASAP, within 20 minutes after patient physical assaults on staff	415 direct care staff at a state mental hospital: pre-post design	Assault Rate: 5 months pre-intervention, 5 months post-intervention	t = 16.47 p < .005	11.65 p < .0001
Mitchell (2000)	42 months after tornado disaster	18 most seriously affected firefighters involved in the body handling of the dead or wounded children: pre-post design	Diagnostic Clinical Interview conducted by 2 mental health professionals screening for 3 symptom clusters of PTSD; pre-treatment and then at follow up 4 months later	X^2=8.1 p<.004	1.81 p=.002
Richards (1999)	3 days after involvement in armed robberies	250 individuals involved in armed robberies: repeated measure design	Impact of Events Scale-Total Score: repeated measures - 3 days & six months post-trauma	t=3.43 p<.05	3.61 p<.0001
Aggregate of studies listed above		Aggregate pool of 1,839 subjects within 7 studies			**Mean Cohen's D** 3.71 p<.0001

*The Assaulted Staff Action Program (ASAP) is a program designed to provide CISM services to staff who have been assaulted by patients.

REFERENCES

American Psychiatric Association (1989). *Treatments of Psychiatric Disorders.* Washington, DC: Author.

Bisson, J.I. & Deahl, M. (1994). Psychological debriefing and the prevention of post traumatic stress: More research is needed. *British Journal of Psychiatry, 165,* 717-720.

Busuttil, W., Turnbull, G., Neal, L., Rollins, J., West, A., Blanch, N., & Herepath, R. (1995). Incorporating psychological debriefing techniques within a brief group therapy programme for the treatment of post traumatic stress disorder. *British Journal of Psychiatry, 167,* 495-502.

Cohen, J. (1977). *Statistical Power Analysis for the Behavioral Sciences.* NY: Academic Press.

Everly, G.S., Boyle, S., & Lating, J. (1999). Effectiveness of psychological debriefing with vicarious trauma: A meta-analysis. *Stress Medicine, 15,* 229-233.

Everly, G.S. & Boyle, S. (1999). Critical Incident Stress Debriefing (CISD): A meta-analysis. *International Journal of Emergency Mental Health, 1,* 165-168.

Everly, G.S., Flannery, R.B. & Mitchell, J.T., (2000). Critical Incident Stress Management (CISM): A Review of the literature. *Aggression and Violent Behavior, 5,* 23-40.

Everly, G.S., & Mitchell, J.T. (1999). *Critical Incident Stress Management: A New Era and Standard of Care in Crisis Intervention (2nd Ed.).* Ellicott City, MD: Chevron.

Everly, G.S. & Piacentini, A. (1999, March). Effects of CISD on stress and trauma symptoms: A meta-analysis. APAA/NIOSH Work, *Stress 7 Health '99 Conference,* Baltimore.

Flannery, R.B. (1999a). Critical Incident Stress Management and the assaulted staff action program. *International Journal of Emergency Mental Health, 1,* 103-108.

Flannery, R.B. (1999b). Treating family survivors of mass casualties: A CISM family crisis intervention approach. *International Journal of Emergency Mental Health, 1,* 243-250.

Flannery, R.B. (1998). *The Assaulted Staff Action Program.* Ellicott City, MD: Chevron.

Flannery, R.B. , Penk, W., & Corrigan, M. (1999). Assaulted Staff Action Program (ASAP) and declines in the prevalence of assaults: Community-based replication. *International Journal of Emergency Mental Health, 1,* 19-22.

Flannery, R.B., Hanson, M.A., Penk, W., Goldfinger, S., Pastva, G., & Navon, M. (1998). Replicated declines in assault rates after the implementation of the ASAP. *Psychiatric Services, 49,* 241-243.

Flannery, R.B., Hanson, M.A., Penk, W., Flannery, G.J., & Gallagher, C. (1995). The Assaulted Staff Action Program: An approach to coping with the after-math of violence in the workplace. In L. Murphy, R. Hurrell, S. Sauter, & Keita (eds). Job *Stress Intervention* 9pp.189-212). Wash, DC: American Psychological Association.

Mitchell, J.T., Schiller, G., Eyler, V., Everly, G. (1999). Community crisis intervention. The Coldenham tragedy revisited. *International Journal of Emergency Mental Health, 1*, 227-236.

Mitchell, J.T., (1983). When disaster strikes...The Critical Incident Stress Debriefing process. *Journal of Emergency Medical Services, 8*, 36- 39.

Mitchell, J.T., & Everly, G.S., (1997). Scientific evidence for CISM. *Journal of Emergency Medical Services, 22*, 87-93.

Mullen, B. (1989). *Advanced BASIC Meta-Analysis*. Hillsdale, NJ: Erlbaum.

Raphael, B., Wilson, J., Meldrum, L., & McFarlane (1996). Acute preventive interventions. In B. van der Kolk, et al. (eds.). *Traumatic Stress* (pp.463-479). NY: Guilford.

Raphael, B., Meldrum, L., & McFarlane, A. (1995). Does debriefing after psychological trauma work? *British Medical Journal, 310*, 1479-1480.

Richards, D. (1999, April). A field study of CISD vs. CISM. Paper presented to the *Fifth World Congress on Stress, Trauma and Coping in the Emergency Services Professions*, Baltimore, Maryland.

Robinson, R. & Mitchell, J. (1995). Getting some balance back into the debriefing debate. *Bulletin of the Australian Psychological Society, 17*, 5-10.

Rosenthal, R. (1979). The "file drawer" problem and tolerance for null results. *Psychological Bulletin, 86*, 638-641.

Watts, R. (1994). The efficacy of critical incident stress debriefing for personnel. *Bulletin of the Australian Psychological Society, 16*, 6-7.

Notes

Section Eleven

CISM
TEAM
FORMATION

SUMMARY OF PROCEDURES TO ESTABLISH CISM TEAMS

A. Determine the need for a team. Count the number of major events that had a serious emotional impact on personnel over the last five years. If the average is five or six a year, a team is indicated. If less, a regional based team would be best for your community. If more, a team is definitely needed in your area.

B. Gain support from the appropriate administration to investigate the need for and the possibility of a team in the administration area. If the boss can be convinced that a team is a good idea and throws support behind it, it is easier to put it together.

C. Talk to local mental health professionals and see if there is interest in this type of community service project.

D. Form a task force of peer support personnel and mental health professionals to develop the team.

E. Gather information about CISM team development. Review what other communities have done. Try to avoid reinventing the CISM wheel.

F. Solicit financial support from agencies and the private sector to cover the costs of training and maintaining the team.

G. Send out applications for team membership. (Several states already have an application process. Review theirs and see if it fits your needs.) Separate professional and peer support applications may be necessary.

H. Review applications and select those who have the best potential to work on the team. Don't promise anyone a place on the team until initial training is complete.

I. Arrange for training of the team. (Sometimes this is done much earlier in the process to assure a timely start up of the team.).

J. Provide training. This should be a minimum of 2 days and should be identical to the training provided to the other CISM teams. *Use only ICISF approved basic course instructors.*

K. Establish the leadership on the team.

L. Develop written operating procedures for the team. *See **CISD: An Operations Manual.***

M. Continue to train the newly formed team with items not covered in the initial training.

N. Set up regular meetings of the team to help maintain the interest and assure proper distribution of information.

O. Review CIS incidents to determine any needs for improvement.

<u>Notes</u>

Section Twelve

CIS
INFORMATION
SHEETS

The following two pages may be reproduced with full permission of the
International Critical Incident Stress Foundation, Inc.

CRITICAL INCIDENT STRESS INFORMATION SHEETS

You have experienced a traumatic event or a critical incident (any event that causes unusually strong emotional reactions that have the potential to interfere with the ability to function normally). Even though the event may be over, you may now be experiencing or may experience later, some strong emotional or physical reactions. It is very common, in fact quite *normal*, for people to experience emotional aftershocks when they have passed through a horrible event.

Sometimes the emotional aftershocks (or stress reactions) appear immediately after the traumatic event. Sometimes they may appear a few hours or a few days later. And, in some cases, weeks or months may pass before the stress reactions appear.

The signs and symptoms of a stress reaction may last a few days, a few weeks, a few months, or longer, depending on the severity of the traumatic event. The understanding and the support of loved ones usually cause the stress reactions to pass more quickly. Occasionally, the traumatic event is so painful that professional assistance may be necessary. This does not imply craziness or weakness. It simply indicates that the particular event was just too powerful for the person to manage by himself.

Here are some common signs and signals of a stress reaction:

Physical*	*Cognitive*	*Emotional*	*Behavioral*
chills	confusion	fear	withdrawal
thirst	nightmares	guilt	antisocial acts
fatigue	uncertainty	grief	inability to rest
nausea	hypervigilance	panic	intensified pacing
fainting	suspiciousness	denial	erratic movements
twitches	intrusive images	anxiety	change in social
vomiting	blaming someone	agitation	activity
dizziness	poor problem solving	irritability	change in speech
weakness	poor abstract thinking	depression	patterns
chest pain	poor attention/ decisions	intense anger	loss or increase of
headaches	poor concentration/memory	apprehension	appetite
elevated BP	disorientation of time, place	emotional shock	hyperalert to
rapid heart rate	or person	emotional outbursts	environment
muscle tremors	difficulty identifying	feeling overwhelmed	increased alcohol
shock symptoms	objects or people	loss of emotional	consumption
grinding of teeth	heightened or	control	change in usual
visual difficulties	lowered alertness	inappropriate emotional	communications
profuse sweating	increased or decreased	response	etc...
difficulty breathing	awareness of	etc...	
etc...	surroundings		
	etc...		

* Any of these symptoms may indicate the need for medical evaluation.
When in doubt, contact a physician.

THINGS TO TRY:

- WITHIN THE FIRST 24 - 48 HOURS periods of appropriate physical exercise, alternated with relaxation will alleviate some of the physical reactions.
- Structure your time; keep busy.
- You're normal and having normal reactions; don't label yourself crazy.
- Talk to people; talk is the most healing medicine.
- Be aware of *numbing* the pain with overuse of drugs or alcohol, you don't need to complicate this with a substance abuse problem.
- Reach out; people do care.
- Maintain as normal a schedule as possible.
- Spend time with others.
- Help your co-workers as much as possible by sharing feelings and checking out how they are doing.
- Give yourself permission to feel rotten and share your feelings with others.
- Keep a journal; write your way through those sleepless hours.
- Do things that feel good to you.
- Realize those around you are under stress.
- Don't make any big life changes.
- Do make as many daily decisions as possible that will give you a feeling of control over your life, i.e., if someone asks you what you want to eat, answer him even if you're not sure.
- Get plenty of rest.
- Don't try to fight reoccurring thoughts, dreams or flashbacks - they are normal and will decrease over time and become less painful.
- Eat well-balanced and regular meals (even if you don't feel like it).

FOR FAMILY MEMBERS & FRIENDS

- Listen carefully.
- Spend time with the traumatized person.
- Offer your assistance and a listening ear if (s)he has not asked for help.
- Reassure him that he is safe.
- Help him with everyday tasks like cleaning, cooking, caring for the family, minding children.
- Give him some private time.
- Don't take his anger or other feelings personally.
- Don't tell him that he is "lucky it wasn't worse;" a traumatized person is not consoled by those statements. Instead, tell him that you are sorry such an event has occurred and you want to understand and assist him.

Appendix

PHASES OF THE AIRLINE MASS DISASTER

Phases of the Airline Mass Disaster

Johanna O'Flaherty

Phases of the Aftermath

Phase I: Mobilization of Team

Identify a clear command structure

Role definitions/boundries

Mechanism in place to resolve conflict

Maintaining support structure

Support for caregivers:

  CISM

Johanna O'Flaherty

Phases of the Aftermath

Phase II: Stabilization

Injured in hospital:

Stabilized or released

Deceased repatriated

Funerals

Memorials

Support for caregivers:

CISM

Johanna O'Flaherty

Phases of the Aftermath

Phase III: Deactivation

Closing

CISM, esp., CISD

Therapeutic time off

Re-integration into workforce

Johanna O'Flaherty

Phases of the Aftermath

Phase IV: Corporate Recovery
Community Recovery

Administrative CISD

Lessons learned vs. blaming

Should have...(Shame)

Executive CISD (contact clinicians)

Public acknowledgment of incident

In-house publications

On-going support for corporate
recovery. EAP's role?

Johanna O'Flaherty

146

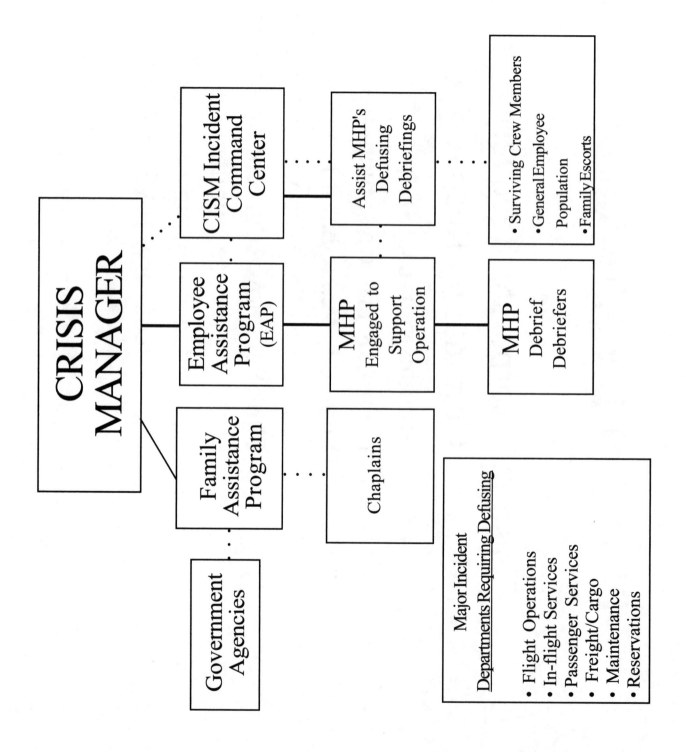